"IN ALL OF ITS HISTORY, NO ONE HAS
EVER MANAGED TO CONQUER
AFGHANISTAN ... NO ONE ... NEVER ..."

Captain Bystrov in the 2005 movie, *9th Company*,
directed by Fedor Bondarchuk

SOVIET AND Mujahideen

UNIFORMS, CLOTHING, AND EQUIPMENT IN THE **SOVIET-AFGHAN WAR**, 1979–1989

ZAMMIS SCHEIN

Schiffer Publishing Ltd ®

4880 Lower Valley Road • Atglen, PA 19310

Library of Congress Control Number: 2016935924

Cover design by Justin Watkinson
Type set in Krasivyi/Akzidenz Grotesk Light
ISBN: 978-0-7643-5115-0
Printed in China

Published by Schiffer Publishing, Ltd.
4880 Lower Valley Road
Atglen, PA 19310
Phone: (610) 593-1777; Fax: (610) 593-2002
E-mail: Info@schifferbooks.com
Web: www.schifferbooks.com

For our complete selection of fine books on this and related subjects, please visit our website at www.schifferbooks.com. You may also write for a free catalog.

Schiffer Publishing's titles are available at special discounts for bulk purchases for sales promotions or premiums. Special editions, including personalized covers, corporate imprints, and excerpts, can be created in large quantities for special needs. For more information, contact the publisher.

We are always looking for people to write books on new and related subjects. If you have an idea for a book, please contact us at proposals@schifferbooks.com.

This book is dedicated to the memory of the Shuravy, enlisted men, NCOs, and officers as well as women volunteers in the Soviet Army and Air Force, in Spetsnaz as well as in Border Guard units deployed in "Afgan." Also, I dedicate this book to the memory of Afghani civilians and mujahid holy warriors, regardless of their nationality, their ethnic, or their religious background, who were wounded, or maimed, or who perished in the Soviet-Afghan war between 1979 and 1989.

CONTENTS

PREFACE

Excerpts from *Zarbalistan: The Traveler's Ultimate Guide to Ariana,*
by Zammis Schein

"... He walked past the outer perimeter security area with a slight limp, he waded through oceans of mud and puddles and he said 'Salaam Bacha' to him. It is supposed to mean 'hello boy' in Dari. He had a big smile on his face and quite unexpectedly he tussled the little boy's thick black hair ..."

The great Soviet/Ukrainian songwriter Yuriy Skitun's song *"Vivat Shuravy–Salam Bacha'"* became an anthem of *Afghantsi*, the Soviet veterans of the Afghan-Soviet War.

"Vivat Shuravy–Salam Bacha" is one of the iconic songs about the war and the lost generation of *shuravy*, which is local Afghani slang word for Soviet soldiers. The word *shuravy* was also adopted by the Soviets and used extensively by troops and veterans alike.

Skitun served in Kandahar between 1979 and 1981. I followed in his footsteps more than two decades later ... Skitun knows what he is talking about. So do I."

Shuravy is a local Dari word for Soviet soldiers. It might as well be regarded as slang, but it was not necessarily interpreted as a pejorative term, unless the Afghans used it with an obvious intent to offend Soviet troops in Afghanistan. *Shuravy* was adopted and often used even by Soviet soldiers themselves.

Obviously, in formal situations they addressed each other by rank and surname, or they added *tovarish* as a prefix to the rank of the other individual, but informally they used either first names, or if they talked to a few of their buddies, they often addressed them as *reebyata*, which means "you guys" in this context.

With the passage of time, *shuravy* was gradually adapted by front-line soldiers and the term was used by the entire lost generation of Soviet youths in the "limited contingent of Soviet forces" serving in *Afgan*. Most of them were conscript soldiers, NCOs, and career officers in the Soviet armed forces. A few of them, like nurses, were civilian volunteers. Their sense of duty, their political idealism, their loyalty to their motherland, their enthusiasm to help the working classes of other nations, their bravery and their self-sacrificing spirit were abused by the communist regime of the Soviet Union on a grand scale.

Over a period of almost nine years until February 15, 1989, namely the formal withdrawal of the last Soviet troops, roughly 15,000 of these brave young kids were killed and over 35,000 of them were maimed and wounded, or suffered irreparable mental harm. Their wounds would never heal. Most of them fell prey to the *Mujahideen*, namely warriors in the holy war, whom they frequently referred to as *dushman*. However, Soviet ranks were also decimated by disease as well as poor sanitary conditions and disastrous medical services.

The term *dushman* was nothing but an ethnic slur and it was used for Mujahid warriors and for any hostile civilians who aided and supported the insurgents. Actually, *dushman* stems from old Persian, where it meant an enemy. It was adopted into the languages of a number of neighboring nations, including Dari and Pashtu, i.e. the two native languages spoken by most people in Afghanistan, and it is a recent loanword in Russian as well. Interestingly enough, in the military slang of combat troops *dushman* was corrupted to *dooh*, which means a spirit, or a ghost in Russian.

Doohy (plural of *dooh*) might be the most appropriate term for an enemy that may appear to be a peaceful civilian in one moment, but may transform itself into an armed combatant in a split second, or vice versa. The Soviets in Afghanistan encountered an enemy that was as elusive as ghosts, an enemy that could blend into the local terrain, as if Mujahideen warriors had been a natural part of the barren hillsides, the rocky mountains, the ruined villages, the dusty roads, or the green fields, rice paddies, poppy fields, cannabis indica plantations, or fruit orchards.

ACKNOWLEDGMENTS

This book would have never been produced in this format and at this specific point in time without the valuable help of a few great people and without the hindrance, or the negligence and ignorance of quite a few other people. I salute those who helped and encouraged me.

Special thanks to my muse; namely to Kati, my wife.

INTRODUCTION

My interest in Soviet and Mujahid militaria started with my first trips to Afghanistan. Over the past ten years and in the course of several tours in *Stan* I fell in love with the country and its peoples and its troubled history. Gradually, with the passage of time and along with the increasing scope of my firsthand experiences with Afghanistan, which is commonly regarded as a notoriously inhospitable country to foreigners, I could gauge the formidable odds against invaders' armies and I started to appreciate the heroism of all soldiers who tried to conquer Afghanistan over the past twenty-four centuries. I started to admire the heroism of successive generations of local peoples whose steadfast resolve to defend their land against foreign intruders posed quite a challenge to Alexander's Macedonian "liberators" of Bactria in 330 BCE and whose descendents repelled two waves of conquering armies of the British Empire in the nineteenth century and "internationalists" in the "limited contingent" of the mighty Soviet forces in the 1980s with equal success.

The history of Afghanistan seems to have repeated itself every time the threat of foreign invaders galvanized local peoples against a common enemy. In true Afghani fashion, the same Mujahid warriors who fought the Soviets in the 1980s and who fought against rival Afghani warlords and who butchered their own countrymen with great fervor and zeal in the 1990s as well as a younger generation of Afghans, namely their sons and their grandchildren, seem to have stood their ground against an international coalition of the United States and ISAF (International Security Assistance Force) nations in the first decade of the twenty-first century again.

Since insurgents fighting against the Afghan government and against the presence of US and ISAF troops on Afghani soil still wear the same clothes and use roughly the same weapons even today, photographs presenting Mujahideen militaria at the time of the Soviet war might as well be used as an illustrated guide to current Afghan insurgent gear. The only major difference between the appearance of an Afghan man, namely a *Mujahid* warrior during the Soviet war and an insurgent fighting ISAF is that the *shemagh*, the omnipresent shawl on the shoulders of the "man in the street,", or hiding the face of insurgents these days was less frequently worn by tribal warriors in the 1980s. This is an oft-disregarded change in local fashion trends and customs. Original photographs suggest that while *shemaghs* were pretty common and were worn regularly even by famous Afghans, like Ahmad Shah Massoud in the field, the emergence of the *shemagh* took place towards the end of the Soviet war and mainly in the late 1990s. Anyway, I used *shemaghs* in chapters when *shemaghs* were present in the underlying original photographs.

I was a civilian teacher in an Afghani girls' school, and while all my efforts were focused on winning the hearts and minds of local people, I started to collect Soviet uniforms and equipment in my free time. I was embedded in the local community, and I was working pretty hard on gaining a certain measure of tolerance, respect, and recognition among the extended families of my students and local people in scenic Pul-e Khumri, Baghlan Province when I first came across local Afghani clothing and military gear that Mujahid warriors used in their relentless struggle against rival local Mujahid warlords and invading troops alike.

This is the kind of collectors' guide that I wished I had had as a greenhorn in those early days, and I trust *Soviet and Mujahideen Uniforms, Clothing and Equipment in the Soviet-Afghan War, 1979–1989* will be interesting and informative for all militaria buffs, collectors, reenactors, airsoft warriors, wargamers, and military historians alike.

I must admit I am not an expert, nor is my collection complete. Anyway, I was at the right place and at the right time to start a Soviet-Afghan war collection, while I was teaching courses in my girls' school in Afghanistan. I love Soviet and Mujahid militaria, and I want to share my collection with all like-minded people. I accumulated my collection in the course of several tours in Afghanistan and in hectic transactions with professional and amateur dealers and sellers in post-Soviet republics and with strangers wasting their invaluable treasures on online auction sites.

One of the big attractions in the beginning, namely in the first few years after the ouster of Taliban from Afghanistan in late 2001, was that Soviet and Mujahid military gear worn and carried by front-line troops and warriors seemed to have remained a niche area of militaria collecting that had not yet been devastated by a tsunami of fakes and frauds. Alas, this is not the case anymore. Unsuspecting collectors these days may easily fall prey to predators selling both perfect replicas and poor quality copies through every conceivable channel of militaria trade.

Soviet and Mujahideen Uniforms, Clothing and Equipment in the Soviet-Afghan War, 1979–1989 is not just a reference book for militaria enthusiasts. I sincerely hope it will be a source of fond memories for *Afgantsi* and even those who fought on the other side.

I wish to pay tribute to the *shuravy*, enlisted men, NCOs and officers as well as women volunteers in the Soviet Army and the Air Force, in Airborne, Spetsnaz as well as in Border Guard units deployed in *Afgan*, to Afghani civilians and Mujahideen holy warriors, regardless of their nationality, or their ethnic, or religious background, who were wounded, or maimed, or who perished in the Soviet-Afghan war between 1979 and 1989.

This book was originally conceived in 2014 to commemorate the twenty-fifth anniversary of the withdrawal of the last Soviet combat troops from the Democratic Republic of Afghanistan on February 15, 1989.

I salute the *shuravy*!

• • •

Soviet and Mujahideen Uniforms, Clothing and Equipment in the Soviet-Afghan War, 1979–1989 is intended to be a reasonably detailed illustrated guide. My main purpose was to give readers a clear visual idea of military uniforms, civilian clothing and equipment that Soviet soldiers and Mujahid warriors wore and carried in Afghanistan in the period between December 1979 and February 1989.

I decided to show weapon accessories, like for example magazines, ammo crates and boxes, holsters, ammo belts and chest rigs worn, or carried by individuals, but I left the small arms and light weapons of the Soviet-Afghan war out of this book as a whole. Virtually all types and makes and models of small arms and light weapons of the Soviets and the Mujahideen in my collection will be documented in great detail, and will be the subject of a future volume.

This is, to my knowledge, the first Soviet and Mujahid militaria collectors' guide that brings old photographs back to life and uses contemporary HQ color photographs to show actual configurations of uniforms and clothing as well as equipment of the *shuravy* and the *doohy* in as near to realistic configurations as is practically possible.

For practical reasons I confined the scope of this book to front-line soldiers, NCOs, and officers in the main combat branches of the Soviet armed forces as well as to Mujahid warriors, actually ordinary Afghans, who were thrust by fate into the midst of a relentless guerilla war against one of the largest regular armies in the world.

I must admit I did not intend to catalogue each and every item of Soviet, or Mujahid military gear. My objectives were significantly more modest than that. I applied photographic evidence as a filter, and I included items that were faithfully documented in period-dated still and moving pictures. Besides, my collection has its own limitations.

Nevertheless, I wanted to present as many items as possible, and I used high-resolution color photographs of all details that Soviet and Afghan Mujahid militaria enthusiasts, historians, or veterans may find fascinating.

Intentionally, I did not venture further than quoting basic identification data for the overwhelming majority of items, and I restrained myself to offering the least possible background information and a few strictly personal remarks relating to a few selected items only.

All dates quoted in descriptions of Soviet uniforms are the pattern date as stated in the official field manuals of the Soviet armed forces. In individual cases, when a manufacturer's date stamp was clearly visible in a photograph, I quoted the date of manufacture in brackets. All items in this book are—to the best of my knowledge—of original Soviet-Afghan war period manufacture. Except for specific items, such as battlefield relics that I collected in Afghanistan myself and genuine vet bringbacks, there is no way of telling whether individual period-dated items were issued to troops serving in Afghanistan, or whether items dated 1989 actually saw field service and combat in Afghanistan, or they were issued to returning troops, only.

Uniforms presented in this book were assembled in configurations confirmed by wartime photos. Except for *dembel* uniforms, which are unique one-off items and which were custom-made by their owners, there is photographic evidence for the combination and configuration of all rank and unit insignia, decorations, and badges displayed on these military uniforms. Actually, in the overwhelming majority of cases such insignia, decorations, and badges came with the same uniforms exactly in the same way they were photographed for this book.

I hereby recognize the bravery and the photographic skills of all the unknown amateur photographers whose snapshots survived and are presented on Soviet veteran sites on the Internet. In the course of the selection of uniform configurations and while designing installations of a wide range of military gear for this book, I relied on their snapshots, and I used wartime photos that were taken, and amateur movies that were shot by Soviet servicemen in the theater of operations as photographic evidence. I wish I could digitally remaster and legally copy their pictures and give proper photo credits to them. Alas, most of them have remained anonymous to me.

All photographs taken for this book are of genuine service-issue, or private-purchase Soviet and Afghan Mujahideen items in my own collection. All types of ammunition, hand grenades, land mines, and signal flares presented in this book were either manufactured as *maket*, or as *uchebny* for training purposes, or they were made inert and deactivated in accordance with the law so that they can never be made to fire again.

Zammis Schein
2016

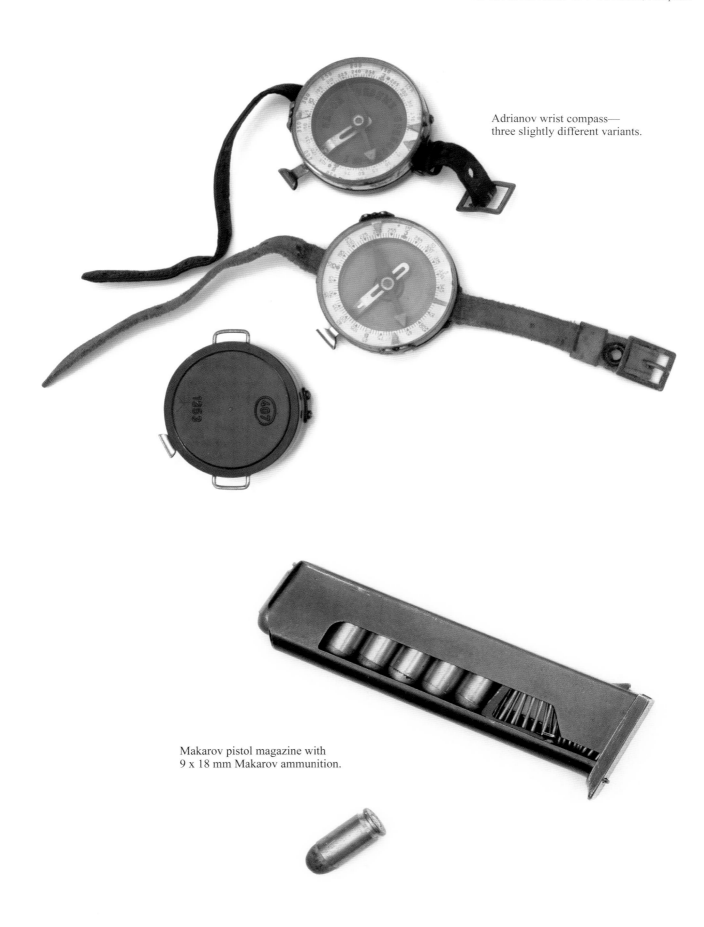

Adrianov wrist compass—
three slightly different variants.

Makarov pistol magazine with
9 x 18 mm Makarov ammunition.

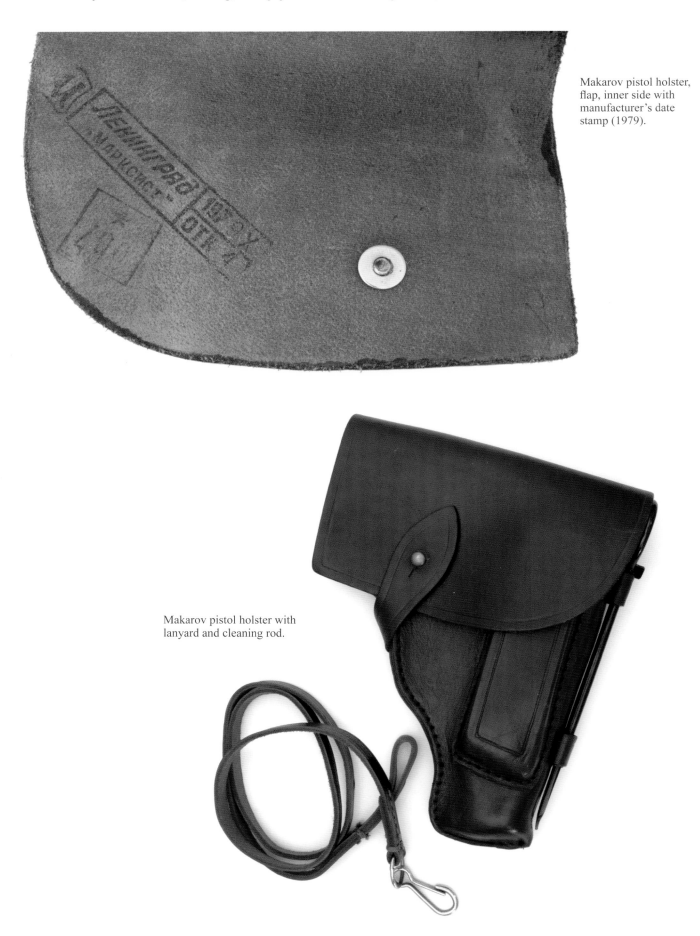

Makarov pistol holster, flap, inner side with manufacturer's date stamp (1979).

Makarov pistol holster with lanyard and cleaning rod.

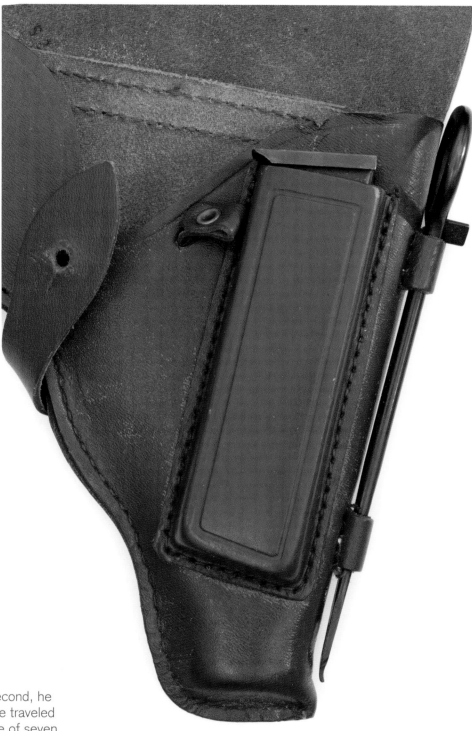

Makarov pistol holster with cleaning rod in leather loops and spare magazine in side pocket.

"He reloaded his pistol in a split second, he flipped the slide catch and the slide traveled forward and picked up the first one of seven rounds of ammo in the newly inserted mag. He learned a clever trick from a local Afghan gunsmith who was a recognized authority on Makarov pistols. He advised the teacher against loading the eighth cartridge in the spare magazine, because it could compress the magazine spring too hard. The round was chambered instantly and he fired …"
— Excerpt from *Zarbalistan* by Zammis Schein

At the end of his tour in Afghanistan.

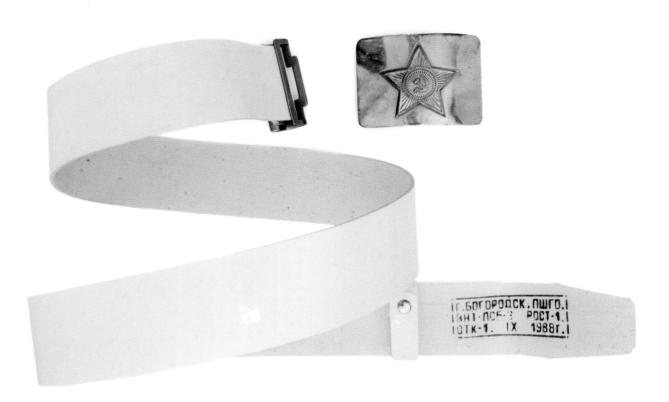

White parade belt with brass buckle. Manufacturer's date (1988) and size stamp is clearly visible.

Ghaloobeeye beret, i.e. blue beret, Soviet airborne. *Dembel*'s customized version with Soviet Army officer's cap badge, side view.

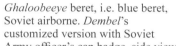

Dembel's customized blue beret, Soviet airborne, red flash with "parachute with two aircraft" airborne pin badge as almost always worn on the left-hand side.

Aiguillette, a braided cord
with or without an ornamental
brass needle.

Quite a few *dembels* (demobilized soldiers, namely conscripts to be discharged, or recently discharged Soviet servicemen) decorated their upgraded and customized uniforms with handcrafted aiguillettes.

VDV airborne troopers preferred parachute cords along the lapel of their single-breasted khaki jackets that were often converted from the standard four-button design to a custom-made, three-button design by removing the top button and reshaping the lapel. Richly ornamented aiguillettes made from parachute cords and custom-made shoulder boards were utilized to further enhance the design.

Sergeant Major (*Starshina*) shoulder board, enlisted men's enameled red star cap badge with "hammer and sickle" symbol placed on aiguillette.

Badges
Top row: civilian College Graduation Badge (arts and humanities faculty).
Middle row: Army EM's Qualifications Badge, Grade 2, Outstanding Soldier badge, Guard Unit badge.
Bottom row: Soldier-Sportsman badge, Grade II, Parachutist Badge, two jumps.

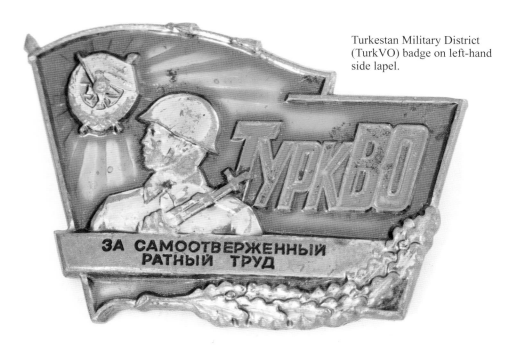

Turkestan Military District (TurkVO) badge on left-hand side lapel.

03. *SPETSNAZ* GRU OFFICER WEARS THE UNIFORM OF A CAPTAIN IN THE SOVIET AIRBORNE

Afghanistan country guide booklet, distributed among Soviet personnel prior to their deployment.

The motto of this book is a quote from Captain Bystrov in the 2005 movie *9th Company* directed by Fedor Bondarchuk. Bystrov made a momentous statement on Afghanistan: " In all of its history no one has ever managed to conquer Afghanistan … No one … Never …"

Military Spetsnaz GRU units and officers, like Captain Bystrov, operated under a thick cloak of secrecy. As a general rule, they were disguised as if they had been in the branch of service and in the specific unit that they were assigned to.

Airborne captain's shoulder board.

04. ARTILLERYMAN IN A DARKER SHADE OF KHAKI
M69 SUMMER FIELD UNIFORM

With *Afganka*, a.k.a. *Panamka* hat, and the daily *Pravda* newspaper.

Gas mask bag. Since NBC (nuclear, biological, chemical) warfare was not an immediate threat in Afghanistan, there was absolutely no need for gas masks. An empty gas mask pouch provided extra stowage capacity for a host of other badly needed items. Manufacturer's date (84) stamp on inner flap.

Map case, inside view.

SSh60 helmet, inside view, four-piece simulated leather liner and manufacturer's date (70) and size stamp. SSh stands for *Stalnoy Shlem*, steel helmet in Russian.

Soviet daily papers from the Afghan war years.
Afghanistan was very rarely mentioned in the news.
Except for the last two years, the horrors of war
were not covered by the Soviet media at all.

Krokodil (Crocodile) was a satirical Soviet
magazine full of fascinating articles and hilariously
funny comics. Afghanistan was not even mentioned
throughout the nine years of war.

05. SOVIET ARMY COLONEL'S M88 *AFGANKA* SUMMER FIELD UNIFORM

With lace-up boots.

Peaked field service cap with earflaps and officer's cap badge. As on all Afghan war-period caps, the two air vents on either side are covered by the ear flaps. The grommets were moved forward on later models, only.

Soviet-Afghan comradeship poster: "Internationalist Mission Accomplished."

06. LIGHTER SHADE OF KHAKI M69 SUMMER FIELD UNIFORM

Worn by a private in a motorized rifle unit in the Soviet army, and wearing an *Afganka* hat prior to his redeployment from Afghanistan.

Uniform buttons were date-stamped on the rear side by the manufacturer.

Sewn-in neck liner, private's red shoulder boards and collar boards bearing the badge of the motorized rifle arm.

Sapogy foot wraps on a pair of
army-issue *Kirza* boots.

Rectangular pieces of cloth, light cotton in the summer
and heavy weight flannel in the winter, were issued to
Soviet enlisted personnel that were worn instead of
socks. Foot cloths were meticulously wrapped around
the feet and were mainly worn with boots.

Kirza is a Soviet-made artificial leather, comprising
several layers of oilcloth saturated with a secret formula
of resin gum. Soviet army heavy-duty EM's boots were
made from *Kirza* with a surface pattern that imitated pig
leather. *Kirza* is an acronym from *Kirovskiy Zavod* (i.e.
Kirov plant), where this unique Soviet artificial leather
was developed and first produced. There must be a
reason why Soviet soldiers casually refered to the *Kirza*
artificial leather material of their boots as *the devil's skin.*

M69 summer field uniform
breeches with straight-cut
pockets and reinforced knees.

07. ARMORED TROOPS' BLACK WINTER UNIFORM TROUSERS

With button-in liner, shearling-lined mittens, EM grade *Ushankah* hat.

Shearling-lined mittens for a tankist with manufacturer's date stamp (85).

30 x 165 (30 mm) linked ammo for the 2A42 gun in the BMP-2 tracked armored fighting vehicle, disintegrating metal links in the background as well as a 5.45 mm round for AK-74 assault rifles for comparison.

Close-up photo of the armored troops' black winter trousers. The button fly with the standard metal hook, the button-in liner as well as the snap fasteners on the thigh pockets are clearly visible.

08. ARMORED TROOPS' BLACK WINTER UNIFORM JACKET

With black, artificial-fur collar and button-in liner.

Tanker's helmets, earlier type and new type side by side, earphones and throat microphones as well as cables and connectors were provided for hooking the helmet up to the on-board intercom.

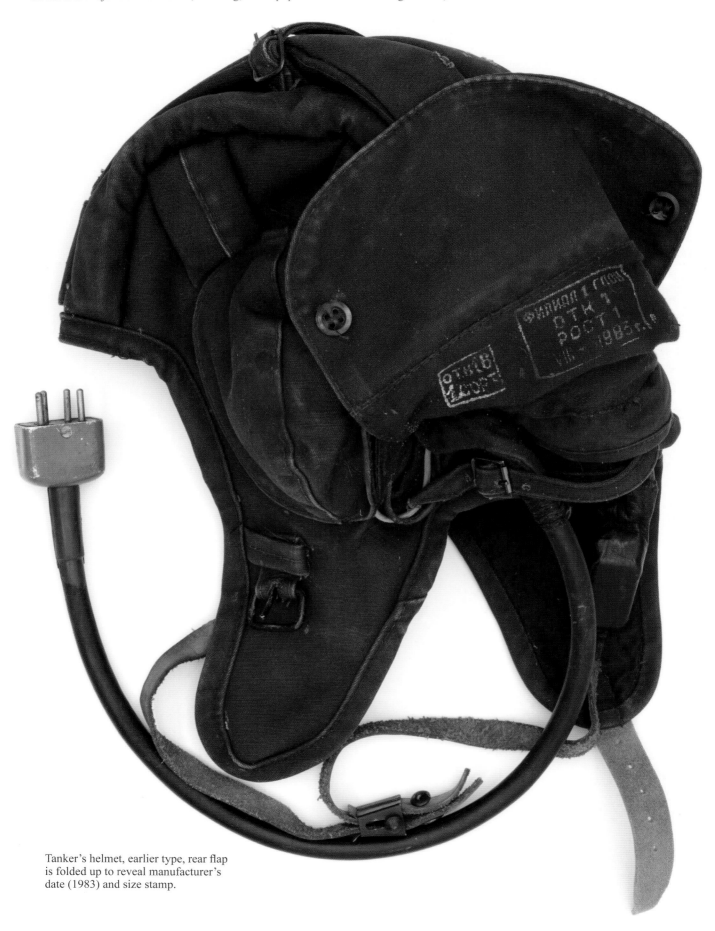

Tanker's helmet, earlier type, rear flap
is folded up to reveal manufacturer's
date (1983) and size stamp.

Detail of tanker's jacket, integral
Makarov pistol holster, and string
lanyard on the left-hand side.

KLMK helmet cover, M69 field uniform, 6B2 fragmentation vest, 14.5 mm ammo for the KPVT heavy machine gun, 7.62 x 39 mm ammo for the AK-47 rifle and 7.62 x 54 mm rounds for the SVD sniper rifle, 5.45 mm ammo on wooden crate and forty five-round RPK-74 magazine for the AK-74 rifle, 12.7 mm linked ammo for the DShK heavy machine gun and 7.62 x 54 mm linked ammo for the PKM light machine gun.

The elastic band along the edge of the hood holds the makeshift helmet cover in place. Slight wear and tear is clearly visible along the brim of the helmet.

The helmet cover is made from the detachable hood of the two-piece KLMK Camouflage Summer Deceptive Coverall uniform. The elongated sewn-on loops allowed to attach additional foliage to the camo material.

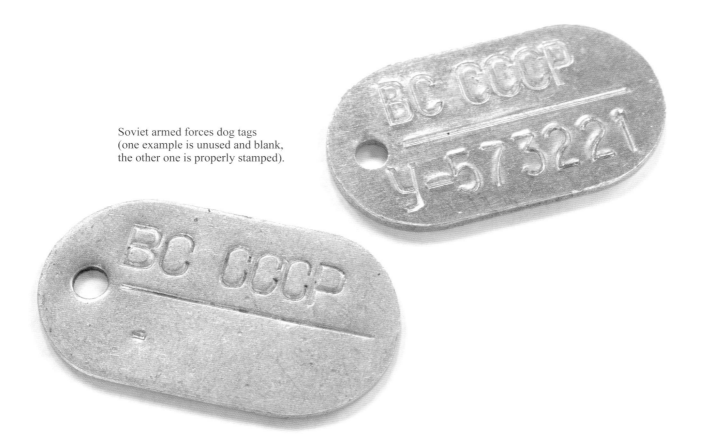

Soviet armed forces dog tags
(one example is unused and blank,
the other one is properly stamped).

"BC CCCP" in Cyrillic stands for "Soviet Armed Forces Union of Soviet Socialist Republics." Since the deployment of a "limited contingent of the Soviet Armed Forces" to Afghanistan was not considered to be a full-scale war, enlisted personnel were not issued dog tags during the Afghan war years. However, the single aluminum dog tag of each officer—and reserve officer—was issued and stamped with his serial number. Soviet dog tags were not issued in pairs, like in the armed forces of the majority of countries. Nor were Soviet tags issued with a regulation string. Only a few Soviet officers actually suspended their tags on a length of rope, or a shoelace and wore it around their necks. The aluminum tags were carried in the small watch pocket of regulation trousers, or were inserted between the pages of Military ID Books. Even custom-made copies of the official tags were quite rare among enlisted personnel. A superstitious fear of the obliteration of their names in case the aluminum tag melted in a fire discouraged hosts of soldiers from using an aluminum medal, or dog tag like their officers. Some carried their personal data on a slip of paper sealed in a spent cartridge case.

Ammo box holding 800-rounds of 7.62 x 54 mm linked ammunition in a belt with starter tab, ready to be used in the nose gun, or the waist gun in an Mi-8 helicopter gunship.

Ammo box for 800-rounds, hinged lid is open to reveal ammo belt folded in two compartments.

23 x 152 mm linked ammo and ammo box for the ZU-23 heavy twin-machine gun.

10. *TANKIST* IN TANKER'S VEST OVER M69 FIELD UNIFORM

With private-purchase motorcycle goggles.

Service-issue tanker's goggles on helmet, as regularly worn by armored crews.

Private purchase motorcycle goggles with sun shield.

11. MAJOR'S SUMMER EVERYDAY UNIFORM

Single-breasted khaki jacket with matching khaki shirt and tie, breeches with red stripes along the outer seams according to his arm of service (armor), and fine leather high boots.

Detail of single-breasted khaki jacket with badges.
Top row: Officer's Skill Level Qualification badge, 1st class.
Bottom row: civilian breast badge awarded to College Graduates of a Mining Institute, Guard Unit badge.

Detail of single-breasted khaki jacket with retired officer's medal ribbons:
Top row: Medal "For Combat Merits"/"For Victory over Germany in the Great Patriotic War 1941-1945"/Medal "For Impeccable Service" – 20 Years.
Middle row: Jubilee Medal "30 Years of the Soviet Army and Navy"/Medal "For the Defense of Moscow"/Medal "Veteran of Armed Forces of the USSR."
Bottom row: Jubilee medal "For Valiant Labour in Commemoration of the 100th Anniversary of the Birth of Vladimir Ilyich Lenin"/Jubilee medal "Forty Years of Victory in the Great Patriotic War 1941–1945."

Khaki peaked cap, red color piping and black cap band in proper arm colors, gilt chin strap, army officer's cap badge, and black plastic visor.

12. OFFICER'S SHIRT SLEEVE ORDER, MAJOR IN ARMORED BRANCH

Major's shoulder board for shirt.

The "Order of the Patriotic War," 2nd Class with award booklet. All surviving WWII veterans were awarded this medal in 1985 during the celebrations of the 40th anniversary of the Great Patriotic War.

Envelopes of letters home from soldier in Afghanistan
with military postal stamps.

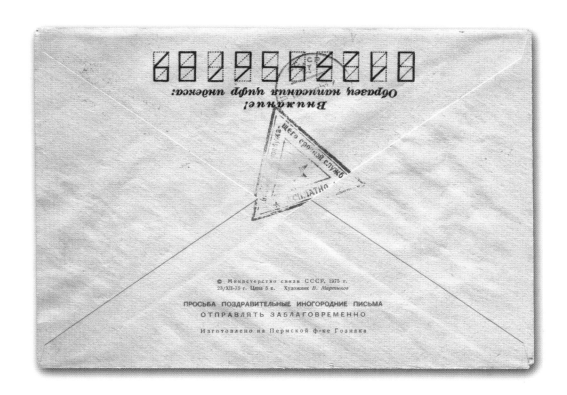

13. WINTER FIELD JACKET WITH FUR COLLAR
Helmet worn on top of *Ushankah* fur hat with EM's "Wreathed Red Star" cap badge.

A Soviet military uniform *ushankah* (literal translation from Russian: hat with ear flaps) is an artificial fur hat made of wool pile with a thick cloth top. Similar to artificial fur collars on M69 and M88 Soviet uniform heavy winter jackets, including the button-in liners of *Afganka*, as well as *Spetsodezhda* and *TTsKO* winter jackets, the EM's *ushankah* was made of a rough, bristlelike pile material that explains why soldiers referred to it as "fish fur." The officers' version was made of a softer and higher quality artificial fur.

An *ushankah* is either worn with earflaps neatly tied on top of the crown of the cap, or with earflaps tied under the chin. The thick fur hat protected its wearer from extreme temperatures and from blunt impacts to the head. Soviet soldiers regularly placed their steel helmets on top of their *ushankah* hats.

Shearling-lined khaki mittens.

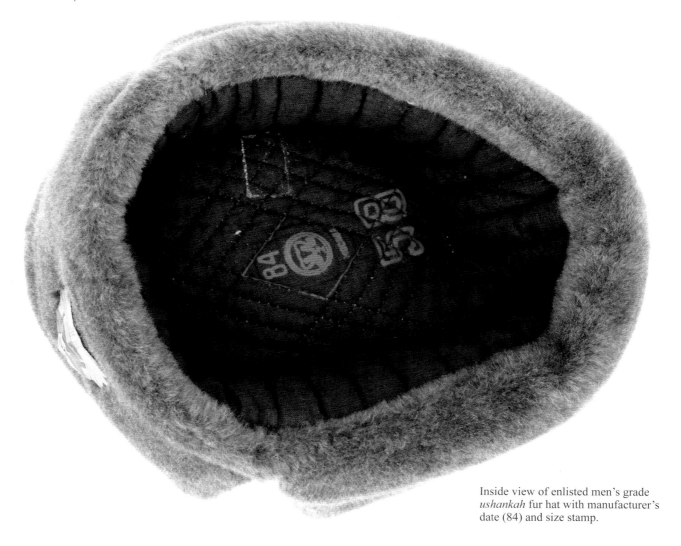

Inside view of enlisted men's grade *ushankah* fur hat with manufacturer's date (84) and size stamp.

SSh68 helmet worn on top of *ushankah* fur hat.
The SSh68 liner was designed to accommodate
the bulky fur hat, which was traditionally worn in
this configuration.

SSh68 helmet riding high on top of the *ushankah* fur hat.
If the chinstrap was not long enough to reach the buckle
on the other side, a length of rope had to be added to it.

14. ARMY SAPPER'S M88 *AFGANKA* SUMMER FIELD UNIFORM

With lace-up boots.

This uniform was acquired in a street market in Pul-e Khumri, Baghlan Province, Afghanistan, in 2011. Elastic bands in the trousers cuffs must be a clever field modification that remained untouched for over two decades.

This army sapper is presented in a *telnyashka* striped T-shirt (sleeveless vest), an enlisted men's grade *ushankah* fur hat with red star badge and a pair of late-war lace-up boots.

Period-dated cigarettes, tobacco, cigarette paper and cigarette
cases, box of matches and lighter.

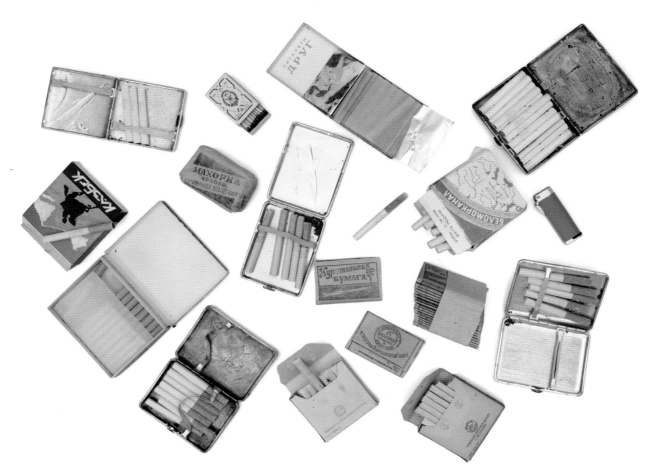

Army issue enameled cups, tin cans for tealeaves,
painted wooden spoon and aluminum spoon.

Mess kit, canteen. The aluminum plate and spoon
are battlefield relics collected in Doshi, Baghlan
Province, Afghanistan in 2008.

15. ARMY SAPPER'S ONE-PIECE KLMK CAMOUFLAGE UNIFORM, WITH 6B2 FRAGMENTATION VEST

With SSh40 steel helmet, and mine probe.

Threaded lower end of mine probe and metal head with two holes for different positions of the spike placed on SSh40 steel helmet.

Bakelite handle of mine probe.

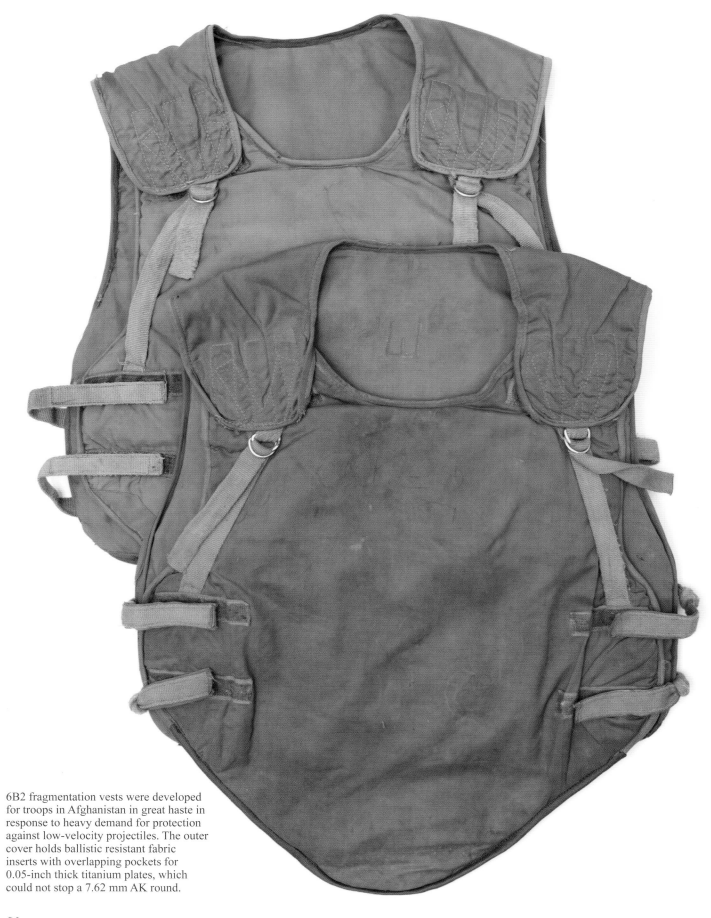

6B2 fragmentation vests were developed for troops in Afghanistan in great haste in response to heavy demand for protection against low-velocity projectiles. The outer cover holds ballistic resistant fabric inserts with overlapping pockets for 0.05-inch thick titanium plates, which could not stop a 7.62 mm AK round.

The front and rear panels of the 6B2 fragmentation vest were held in place by webbing straps and double D-ring fasteners on the shoulders as well as two velcro straps on either side.

BATTLEFIELD RELICS

Militaria items collected in specific battlefields, or in areas and towns that changed hands several times in fierce fighting between well known and documented enemy forces have always been regarded as prized collectibles for veterans and later generations of collectors worldwide.

However, in Afghanistan, the whole country was a battlefield for more than a decade and virtually every square inch of Afghan soil changed hands several times between the Soviets and the Mujahideen, or among numerous Mujahid factions and warlords, respectively. Since each belligerent party used mainly Soviet-made weapons and ammunition, there is no way of telling whether a rare item collected in Afghanistan today was left behind by the Soviets, or by insurgents.

The rusty shell of an SSh60 helmet was recovered in 2011 by brave EOD troops from a minefield in Baghlan Province that had been inaccessible for over two decades. It's more than likely that the helmet once belonged to a Soviet soldier, or to a conscript in Afghan government service. Except for a series of posed photographs of an infamous, non-native guerilla leader in Afghanistan who was wearing a South Korean-made ballistic nylon fiber helmet, which was based on the US M1 pattern and which was sold to several countries but mainly to Iraq, there is no known photographic evidence that confirms the use of Soviet, or any other steel helmets by Mujahideen warriors.

This battered Soviet tanker's helmet once belonged to a *chapandaz*, a local champion Buzkashi rider, the winner of quite a few games, including the Buzkashi event in January 2011, in Baghlan Province. In Buzkashi, each tough man wants to grab, and to hold on to a headless carcass of a goat and to prove his wits, his strength, and his horsemanship; in other words, his superiority over other males, also in this way.

The unexploded F1 hand grenades as well as the spoons and pull rings of assumedly spent F1s were picked up along the road to Mazar-e Sharif, Balkh Province. The rusty shovel blade, stamped 1975 (1978?) and with the manufacturer's "three pine trees" logo and OTK (quality control) proof may have belonged to a vehicle-mounted pioneer tool kit, or to a sapper's tool set. It was found in 2011 near Pul-e Khumri, Baghlan Province by local people who were eager to make a modest contribution to the fledgling Soviet-Mujahid militaria collection of their daughters' English teacher.

16. ARMY SAPPER'S M69 FIELD UNIFORM AND 6B3 FRAGMENTATION VEST

With SSh60 steel helmet, with *KZS* fabric cover, mine probe, IMP mine detector, and minefield marker flags.

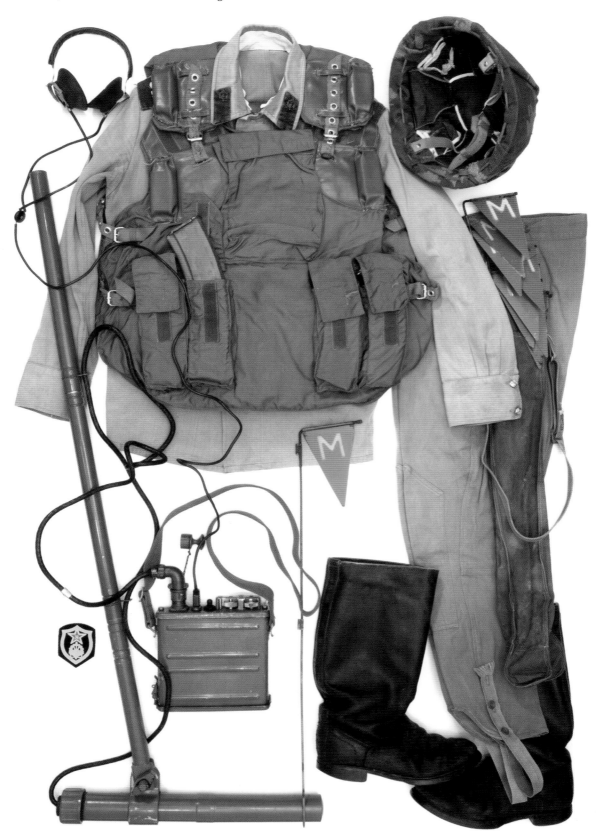

SSh60 steel helmet with a makeshift KZS loose-weave cotton fabric cover, which is assumedly cut from a KZS camo uniform. The shoestring that holds the piece of cloth, which is tucked under the helmet liner, is clearly visible.

Minefield marker flags made of sheet metal in matching canvas bag.

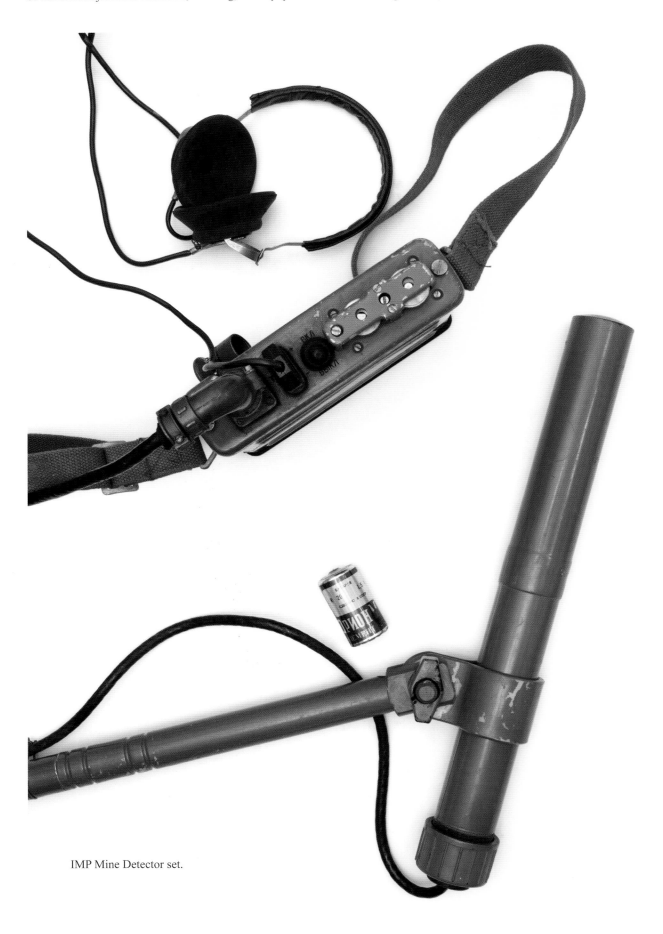

IMP Mine Detector set.

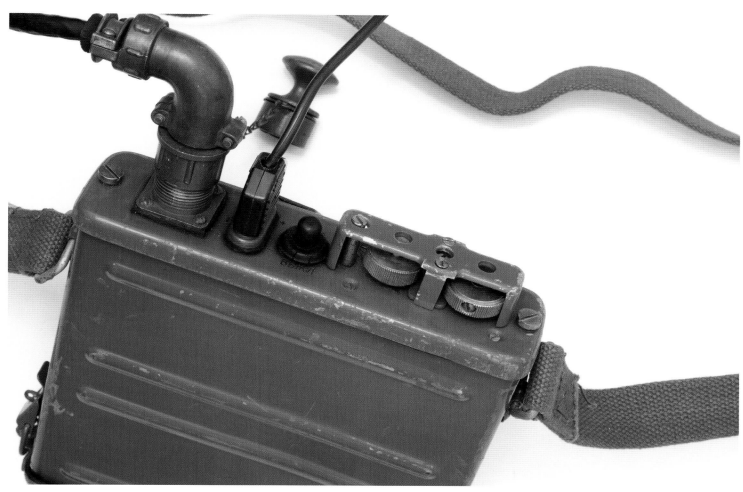

IMP Mine Detector. The receiver and transmitter assembly/control unit has a screw-locked connector on the extension cable to the mine detector head (left) and a two-pole plug on the cable to the headset (second from left), an on-off switch (middle), and sensitivity control knobs (right).

Original, Soviet-made ORION brand 1.5 volt battery. The IMP uses four D-size batteries.

17. ARMY CONSTRUCTION TROOPS – STROYBAT *(STROYTELNY BATALYON)*, SUMMER OUTFIT

M69 uniform, *Pilotka* cap, combat engineer's spade.

Corporal's M69 jacket with a sewn-in collar liner. Using a *podvorotnichok*, undercollar (or a collar liner in Russian), was a longstanding tradition in the Soviet military. A narrow piece of white fabric was folded over and ironed, in less frequent cases a factory-made collar liner was purchased in the military store on base, and sewed onto the inner side of the collar of each field uniform jacket. Undercollars were supposed to be replaced on a daily basis and clean ones had to be attached with large stitches in the evenings before the lights in the barracks were switched off. The *podvorotnichok* in every soldier's coat was inspected in the mornings and army regulations were strictly enforced.

Corporal's shoulder board on his M69 jacket with a
sewn-in collar liner, Army Engineer/Construction
Troops' subdued (green painted) "bulldozer over
circular saw, superimposed on anchor and lightning"
badge on matching black collar board.

Army EM's Qualifications Badge, Grade 3,
Outstanding Soldier badge, Excellence in Military
Construction badge.

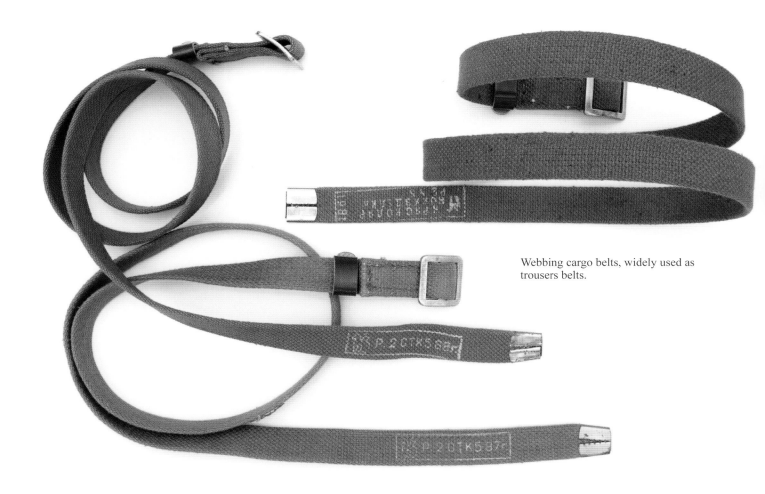

Webbing cargo belts, widely used as trousers belts.

18. ARMY CONSTRUCTION TROOPS – STROYBAT, WINTER OUTFIT

M69 uniform, white flannel undergarments, *Telograykah* (body warmer) cotton wool padded jacket, construction troops' hardhat.

Hardhat inscribed with STROYTEL (literally: builder).

Hammer.

Hardhat, inside view, suspension and chinstrap.

19. PIPELINE CONSTRUCTION TROOPS' SIMULATED LEATHER TWO-PIECE UNIFORM

Burlap helmet cover, with truck tire on rim.

Burlap helmet cover with truck tire on rim.

Entrenching tool and E-tool carrier with belt loops.

Pipeline Construction Troops'
simulated leather jacket.

Pipeline Construction
Troops' simulated leather
trousers, distinctive thigh
pocket on right side and
reinforced knees.

20. ONE-PIECE KLMK CAMOUFLAGE UNIFORM, WITH SOVIET-MADE *MOCKBA* BRAND SNEAKERS

Three-cell Chinese-made chest rig, with *NSP* smoke grenade/ground signal patron on shoulder strap.

Peaked field service cap with earflaps, enlisted men's subdued (painted green) cap badge, front view.

One-piece KLMK Camouflage Summer Deceptive Coverall uniform, front view. The (theoretically) reversible KLMK uniform had a subdued version of the same "stair step" camouflage design printed on a grid pattern on the opposite side.

One-piece KLMK Camouflage Summer
Deceptive Coverall uniform, rear view,
convenient "drop seat" design with wide
opening along the waistline and
buttoned closure.

21. VDV TROOPER'S TWO-PIECE KLMK UNIFORM

Mabuta jacket, three-cell Chinese-made chest rig, Puma shoes, and an R-392 tactical two-way radio with headset.

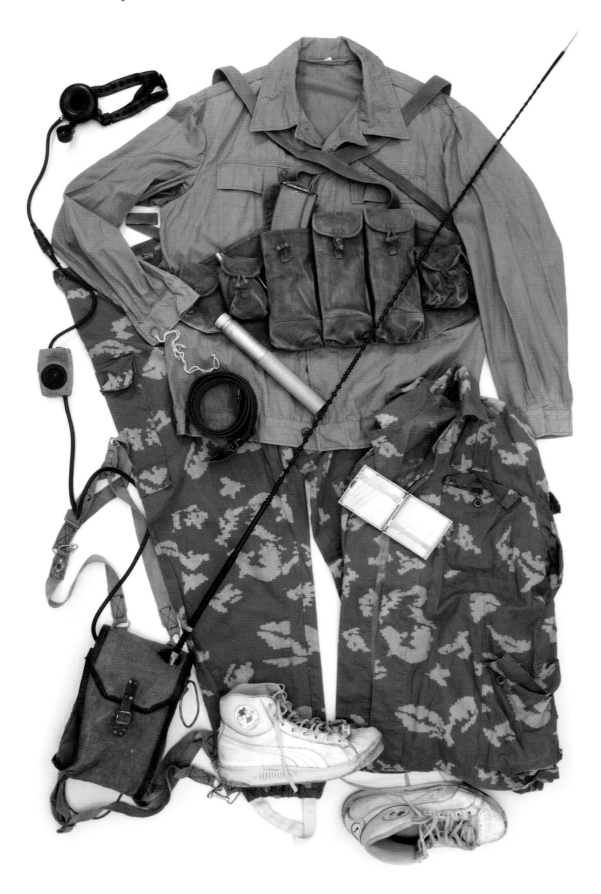

R-392 small manpack transceiver with the headset assembly comprising just one earphone and a cheek microphone.

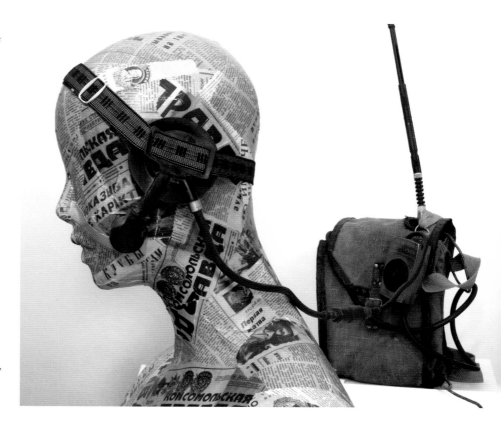

A pair of R-392 radios; the control box with a large dial is installed on the headset cable. The antenna is constructed of a series of aluminum beads that are strung on a flexible steel cable. The antenna beads are held in place by a spring, which may be released easily and the antenna may be rolled up for easy storage within the canvas shoulder bag.

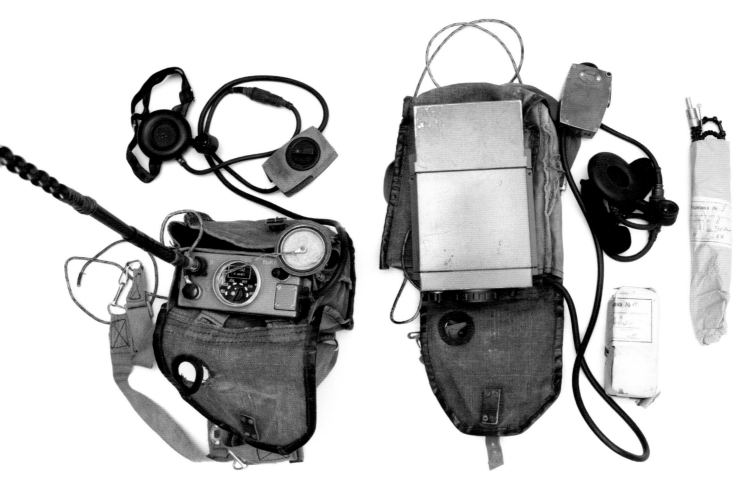

Jacket of the two-piece
KLMK uniform, front view.

KLMK jacket with detachable
hood, rear view. The hood
was often used as a makeshift
camo helmet cover.

Trousers of the two-piece
KLMK uniform, front view.

Cargo pocket on trousers,
two-piece KLMK uniform,
side view.

22. TANKER'S SAND-COLOR, LIGHT SUMMER UNIFORM

Worn off-duty, with ankle boots, while listening to a distant radio station on the RIGA 103 transistor radio.

Tanker's sand-color, light summer uniform, close-up view of cloth "armored forces" chest insignia as well as snap fasteners on chest pockets.

Ankle boots and a pair of heavy-duty wool socks. Enlisted personnel were issued sapogy foot wraps to be worn with their heavy service-issue high boots. However, officers' socks and private purchase stockings often found their way into the hands of enlisted personnel, especially those who wore ankle boots, or sneakers.

One-row hole-grommet belt, originally intended for securing the front and the rear panels of the 6B4 fragmentation vest.

23. TRAFFIC CONTROL MILITARY POLICEMAN IN LIGHT-SHADE SUMMER OKZK UNIFORM

Full *Regulator* (traffic controller) kit with hand-painted SSh60 helmet, and military police *Patrul badge (occasionally worn by servicemen, but not necessarily by military policemen, who were assigned to street patrol duty).*

SSh60 *Regulator* (traffic controller) helmet, hand-painted locally, as always, with a red star on front and the Cyrillic P (pronunciation "R") for *Regulator* painted on three sides of the helmet.

Regulator helmet placed on summer OKZK uniform.

OKZK suits were impregnated against chemical agents and were intended for NBC scenarios, only. Nevertheless, they surfaced here and there. This complete set, including the uniform, the fabric of which does not appear to have been impregnated, the shoulder boards as well as the sleeve patches on either side, where the letter "K" stands for *komandantskaya sluzhba*, i.e. commandant service, and the regulator gear, arrived from the arsenal of a small Soviet garrison exactly the way it is presented here.

Inside view of SSh60 *Regulator* helmet placed on summer OKZK uniform.

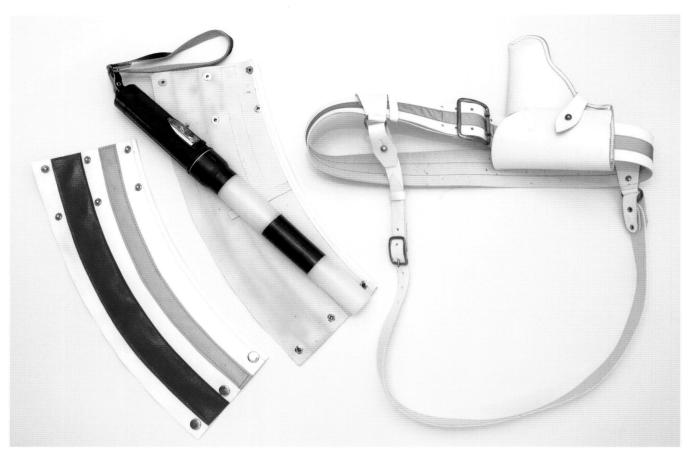

Regulator (traffic controller) detachable simulated leather cuffs with distinctive red and reflective strips and snap fasteners, battery-operated illuminated traffic control baton (left), "Sam Browne"-type belt with reflective strip along its entire length, matching white shoulder strap, and white Makarov pistol holster (right).

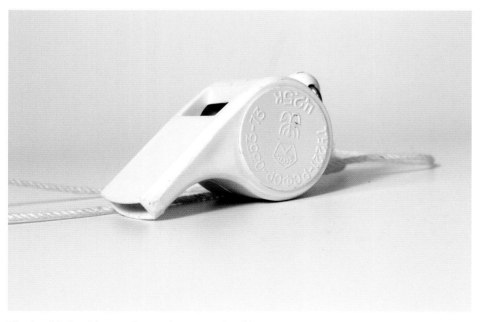

Plastic whistle with manufacturer's specs on its side.

Soviet-made 1.5 volt D-cell, light bulb in plastic housing, illuminated section of the traffic control baton, handle with wrist strap, switch and battery compartment.

24. TRAFFIC CONTROL MILITARY POLICEMAN IN PIPELINE TROOPS' BLACK SIMULATED LEATHER UNIFORM

Full *Regulator* kit, with hand-painted SSh40 helmet.

SSh40 *Regulator* (traffic controller) helmet, hand-painted locally, as always, with a red star on the front, red stripes on either side and the Cyrillic P (pronunciation "R") for *Regulator* painted on the rear of the helmet.

"Sam Browne"-type belt with a reflective strip along its entire length, matching white shoulder strap and white Makarov pistol holster, detachable simulated leather cuffs with distinctive red and reflective strips and snap fasteners. The red and white reflective (cat eye) disk is missing from the shoulder strap. It was not necessarily worn in combat zones.

SSh40 *Regulator* (traffic controller)
helmet, rear view.

SSh40 *Regulator* (traffic controller) helmet,
inside view with paint marks on the rim of
the helmet.

25. MUJAHID COMMANDER, US M65 JACKET, *SHEMAGH* (SHAWL), AHMAD SHAH MASSOUD "PORTRAIT RUG"

With Soviet NCO/Officer's belt, and US M51 trousers. The rug is handmade and was purchased in a street market in Mazar-E Sharif, Balkh Province, Afghanistan, in 2008.

The *pakol* hat became virtually synonymous with the Northern Alliance's holy war against the Soviets all over the world.

US M65 jacket, which was frequently worn by Mujahideen commanders, including Massoud. The collar with label bears a DSA contract number that suggests the year of manufacture was 1970.

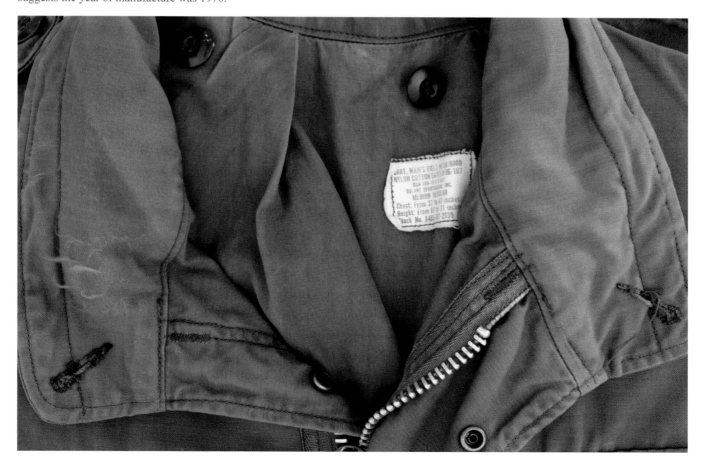

Qahraman Meli
Afghanistan Ahmad
Shah Massoud on a
mass-produced
Iranian portrait rug.

"... The placement of the image of Qahraman Meli Afghanistan Ahmad Shah Massoud on a mass-produced Iranian portrait rug over his desk lent legitimacy to his title and adorned his office in true Afghani style. Qahraman Meli Afghanistan means the Great Champion of the Afghan Nation and is the most frequent title that is used when Ahmad Shah Massoud, a Mujahid commander, a warlord, and a key figure in the Northern Alliance is mentioned. Massoud earned his byname Shir-e-Panjshir, which means the Lion of Panjshir Valley for his bravery and heroism in his decade-long struggle against Soviet occupation and influence. Literally, his highly recognized nickname means "the lion of five lions" and is a rhyming play on Panjshir, i.e. the name of the valley, which means "five lions" in Dari.

He was murdered by Al-Qaeda suicide bombers, who disguised themselves as a TV crew just one day before 9/11. Massoud was posthumously recognized by the new government as Afghanistan's national hero. His portraits on billboards, self adhesive stickers and photographs can be found in the most unlikely places all over Afghanistan ..." — excerpt from *Zarbalistan* by Zammis Schein

Portraits of Ahmad Shah Massoud on a poster and a postage stamp, with *pakol* hat worn in the distinctive Ahmad Shah Massoud style.

99

26. M88 *AFGANKA* UNIFORM

With SSh68 steel helmet and load-bearing shoulder harness in light summer battle order. The orange-colored *Apteka* NBC first aid kit is carried in the left sleeve pocket of the jacket.

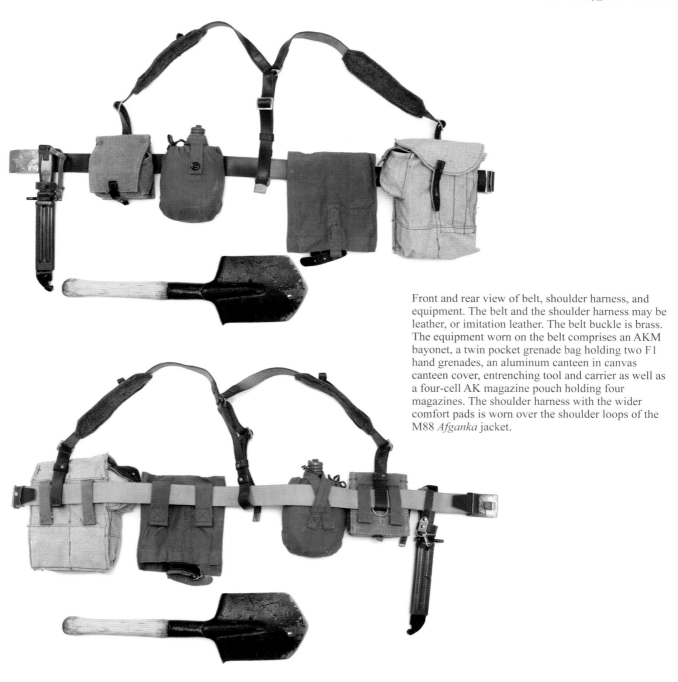

Front and rear view of belt, shoulder harness, and equipment. The belt and the shoulder harness may be leather, or imitation leather. The belt buckle is brass. The equipment worn on the belt comprises an AKM bayonet, a twin pocket grenade bag holding two F1 hand grenades, an aluminum canteen in canvas canteen cover, entrenching tool and carrier as well as a four-cell AK magazine pouch holding four magazines. The shoulder harness with the wider comfort pads is worn over the shoulder loops of the M88 *Afganka* jacket.

Inside view of the SSh68 steel helmet with the manufacturer's size and date (85) stamp.

27. SOVIET ARMORED TROOPS IN THE FIRST FEW DAYS OF THE INVASION OF AFGHANISTAN, IN LATE DECEMBER 1979

Long, dark brownish-grey greatcoat with an Ushankah fur hat, SSh40 steel helmet with four-point "Y" chinstraps, light winter battle order.

Greatcoat with grey canvas liner in upper half. The front of the greatcoat is plain with no buttons visible. It has metal hooks and loops that are mounted on reinforced circular patches made of the same heavy-duty material.

Twin pocket grenade bags holding two F1 hand grenades, each. The manufacturer's date stamp (1982) is clearly visible on the inner flap.

Early five-cell AK-47 magazine pouch with oiler and field cleaning and repair tool set in black metal tube.

SSh40 steel helmet with four-point "Y" chinstraps, inside view.

SSh40 steel helmet, detail four-point suspension and liner, the manufacturer's size and date stamp (58) is clearly visible.

28. WINTER CAMOUFLAGE SUIT

Lightweight white two-piece suit. Jacket with hood has integrated "trigger finger" mittens. The trousers are secured around the waist with a string, and normally worn outside the boots.

Jacket with hood (detail).

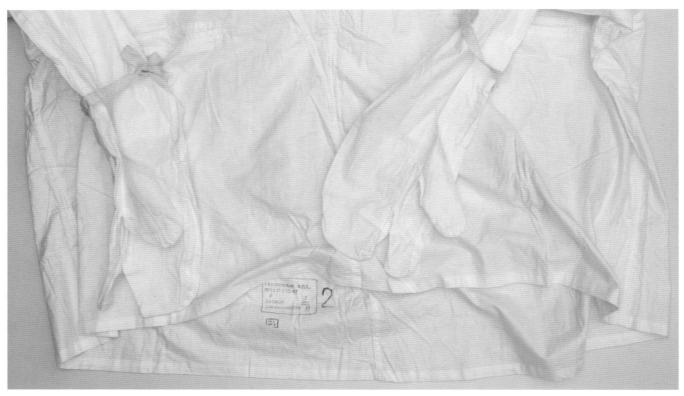

The manufacturer's size and date stamp (77) on the inner rear section of the jacket.

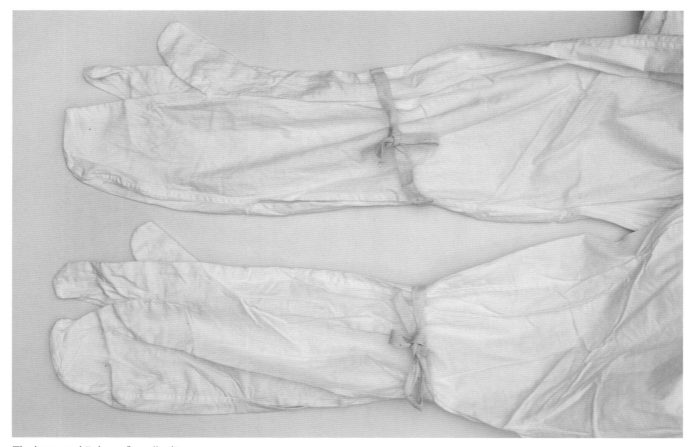

The integrated "trigger finger" mittens are an extension of the sleeves.

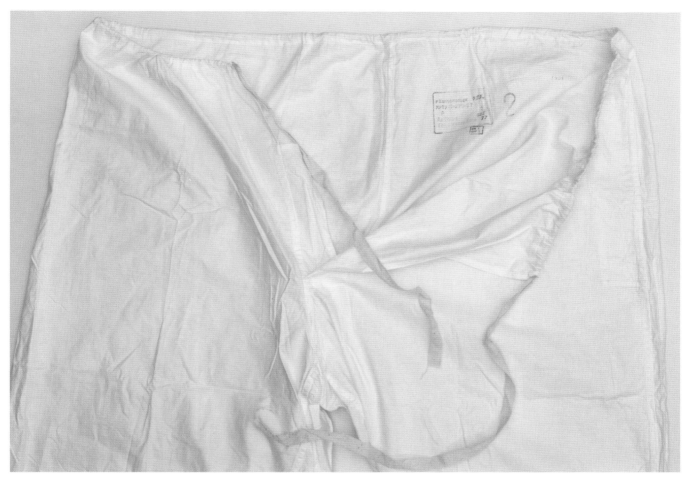

The trousers are secured around the waist with a string.

29. TTSKO THREE-COLOR CAMOUFLAGE UNIFORM

Matching *TTsKO* peaked hat with earflaps, 6B3 fragmentation vest, lace-up boots.

TTsKO peaked hat with earflaps, officer's badge attached with two pins, that—like in the case of all other cap badges—are folded in opposite directions. Two vent holes on either side are hidden by the earflaps.

6B3 fragmentation vest, rear view and front view. The large cargo pocket on the back provided additional stowage capacity for a host of useful item, although "buddy help" was badly needed to gain access to the contents of the rear pocket.

6B3 fragmentation vest, front view. Pads on the shoulders and next to the armpits were mounted on the green simulated leather-reinforced areas to hold rifle slings and the straps of other pieces of equipment in place. The bellows-type chest pocket as well as mag pouches along the waistline of the vest were easily accessible.

30. 6B3 FRAGMENTATION VEST

Ballistic-resistant fabric inserts with overlapping pockets for ¼-inch-thick titanium plates on the front, and for ¹⁄₁₆-inch-thick titanium plates on the rear.

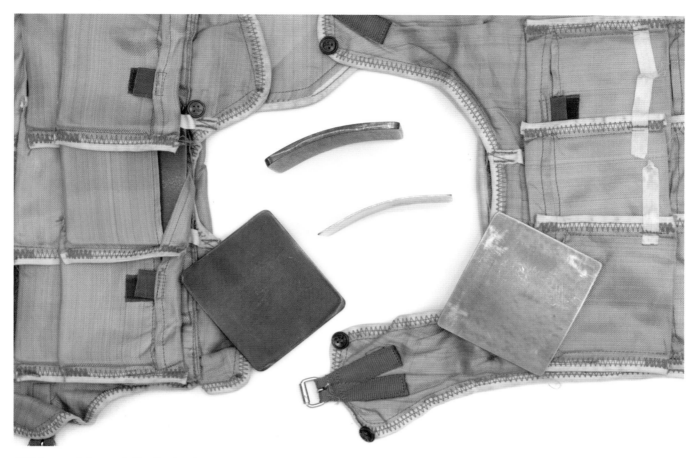

6B3 fragmentation vest. The front and rear dual-layer ballistic resistant fabric inserts, which provided a much greater level of protection against low-velocity projectiles, are folded flat. The outer cover holds ballistic resistant fabric inserts with overlapping pockets for ¼-inch thick titanium plates on the front side, which could stop an AK round. The ¹⁄₁₆-inch thick titanium plates of the earlier 6B2 vest were retained on the rear side.

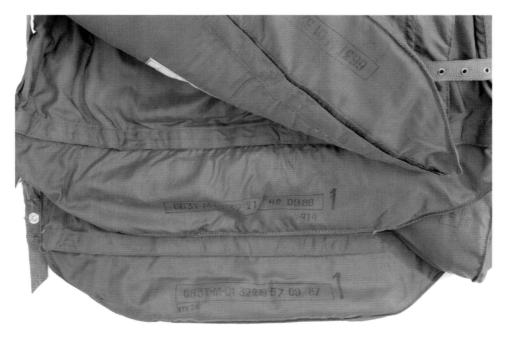

Detail of lower front and rear sections of two 6B3 fragmentation vests with the manufacturer's date stamps (88 and 87 respectively) on the inner rear panels, below the Velcro closure.

113

31. SOVIET AIRBORNE *DYESANTNYK* IN TTSKO SUMMER UNIFORM, WITH TROUSERS SUSPENDERS THREADED THROUGH SLITS IN THE BLOUSE

TTsKO summer uniform, inside view of the blouse. The integral Makarov pistol holster and the trousers suspenders threaded through two front slits and one rear slit in the blouse are clearly visible.

TTsKO summer uniform, blouse, (detail), the manufacturer's size and date (89) stamp is clearly visible on the inner front panel below the pistol holster.

TTsKO summer uniform, blouse, (detail), slit in the front panel for trousers suspenders.

TTsKO summer uniform, blouse, (detail), white buttons along the collar were intended for a collar liner, which is a unique field modification. Normally, collar liners were sewn in with large and loose stitches so that they can be removed easily and replaced with clean ones regularly.

Trousers suspenders went through slits in the front panels and were held by two "D" rings on either side of the trousers' waist.

TTsKO summer uniform, blouse, (detail), cargo breast pocket above the slit in the front panel for trousers suspenders.

TTsKO three-color camouflage winter jacket. Except for the camo material, the cut is like the M88 *Afganka* winter jacket. The inner flap is intended for the button-in liner.

TTsKO three-color camouflage winter jacket, (detail), the manufacturer's size and date (89) stamp is clearly visible on the inner flap for the button-in liner.

TTsKO three-color camouflage winter jacket, (detail), captain's shoulder board, field version with "subdued," i.e. green painted small stars, cargo breast pocket.

Signal flare, 30 mm, color coded screw cap.

Signal flare, (detail), color coded screw cap, with distinctive, embossed "L" shape marking of green flares for easy handling in the dark, the pull ring and the string attached to the fuse are clearly visible.

33. SOVIET AIRBORNE *DYESANTNYK* IN TTSKO WINTER UNIFORM

With trousers, knitted wool Balaclava hood, knitted wool sweater, knitted wool gloves, and lace-up boots.

TTsKO winter trousers with suspenders, (detail), rear view, cargo pockets on both sides.

TTsKO winter trousers, (detail), button fly and metal hook, as almost always on Soviet trousers.

TTsKO winter trousers, (detail), left side view, two-cell cargo pocket to hold two AK-74 magazines.

34. SOVIET AIRBORNE (VDV) SENIOR LIEUTENANT IN SUMMER EVERYDAY UNIFORM

Single-breasted, khaki jacket with matching khaki shirt and tie, trousers with blue stripes along the outer seams according to his arm of service (airborne).

Single-breasted khaki jacket with decorations and badges (detail):
Top row: "Outstanding internationalist" military service in Afghanistan, also known as the "Handshake medal."
Second row: "Order of the Patriotic War," 2nd Class, "Order of the Red Star."
Third row: Officer's Skill Level Qualification badge, 2nd Class.
Bottom row: "GTO"/Prepared for Labor and Defense/badge, Parachutist Badge for 100+25 jumps, Military Academy Graduation badge, Guard Unit badge.

Single-breasted khaki jacket with decorations and badges (detail):
Top row: Medal "For Combat Merits," Medal "For Bravery," Medal "For Impeccable Service," 3rd Class – 10 Years, Jubilee medal "70 Years of the Armed Forces of the USSR."
Bottom row: Soldier-Sportsman badge, Grade I.

Khaki peaked cap, blue color piping and blue cap band in proper arm colors, gilt chinstrap, Air force/Airborne officer's cap badge and black plastic visor.

35. SOVIET AIRBORNE (VDV) SENIOR LIEUTENANT SHIRT SLEEVE ORDER

With Pilotka cap with blue piping, and air force/VDV officer's cap badge, and personal identification documents.

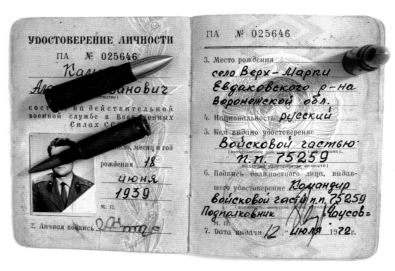

Artillery *proporshik*'s (warrant officer's) Military ID card.

Military ID card (detail), registration of service-issue Makarov pistol.

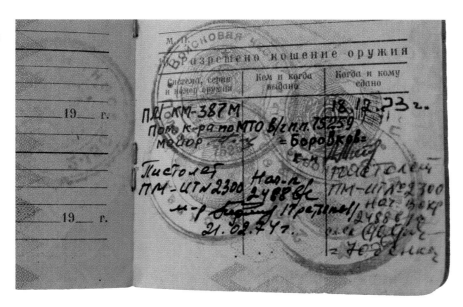

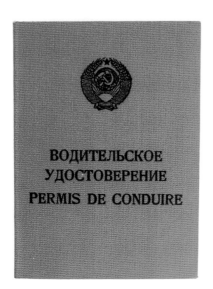

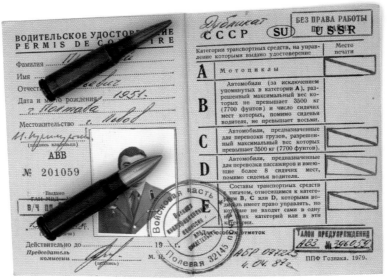

"International" military driver's license of an armored officer on overseas deployment.

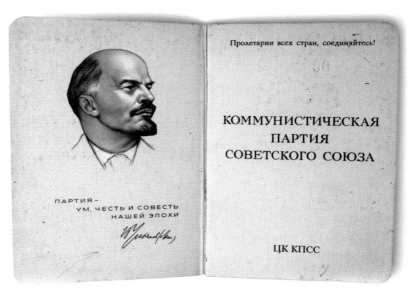

Air Force officer's Communist Party membership card.

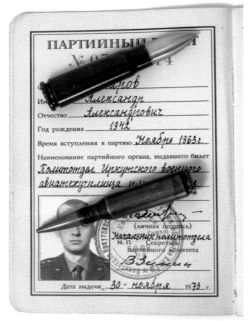

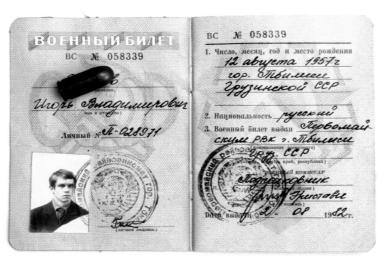

Officer's Military ID card.

Service passport and Communist Membership Card of a Soviet Army (Signal Corps) officer. (inside view of the photo identification pages).

A service passport was issued prior to the deployment of an NCO, or an officer. Enlisted personnel used their military ID booklets, only.

36. *CHAPAN* – AFGHAN *KAFTAN*

Chapan – Afghan *kaftan*, close-up, richly ornamented
collar with brown corduroy lining.

Chapan – Afghan *kaftan*,
(detail), long sleeve.

Chapan – Afghan *kaftan*,
(detail), side slit design.

37. MUJAHID WARRIOR IN *SHALWAR KAMEEZ*

Pakol hat, shemagh, plastic slippers, and a Chinese-made chest rig to hold loose rounds for a SMLE Rifle.

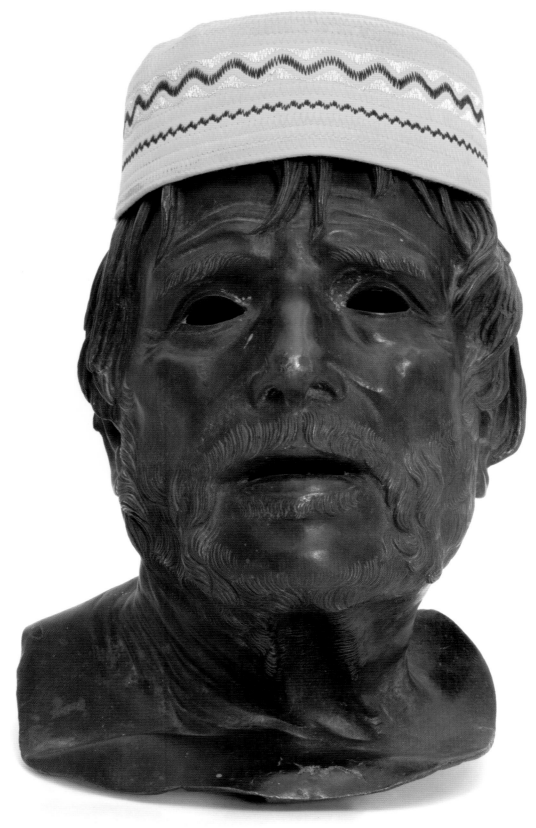

Embroidered *kufi* hat. Geometric pattern.

Embroidered *kufi* hat.
Floral pattern.

Kufi hat. Plain design.

Chinese–made chest rig, originally intended for the ten-round stripper clips of the Chinese Type 56 carbine (SKS) rifle. Although SMLE No1 Mk.III rifles were designed to be loaded with five-round stripper clips, most Afghan warriors fed single rounds of .303 ammunition down into the slot in the bridge and pressed down individual rounds into the magazine by the thumb (*Note*: an empty magazine of the British SMLE rifle was not supposed to be ejected and replaced with a full one, but the same magazine was reloaded and used constantly). The otherwise removable SMLE mag in the photo is displayed separately for demonstration purposes, only. The pockets of this Chinese chest rig for the Type 56 carbine (SKS) are not wide enough to hold Lee-Enfield stripper clips, but in Mujahideen hands they held loose rounds of .303 ammunition. The waxed canvas walls of the tenth pocket on the right-hand side could hold bandages, or—in rare and isolated cases—a small quantity of hash-hash, and matches wrapped in a piece of oil-cloth.

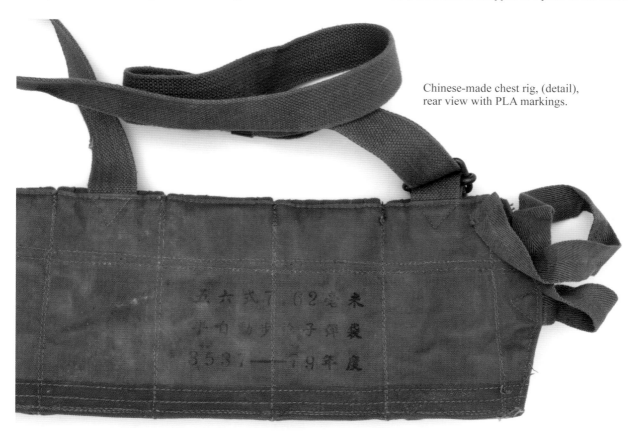

Chinese-made chest rig, (detail), rear view with PLA markings.

38. *SHALWAR KAMEEZ*

With plastic slippers.

The *shalwar* is a pair of loose-fitting pajama-like, *tapered* trousers. The *shalwar* is roomier at the top and somewhat narrower towards the ankle. The *shalwar* is tightened around the waist with a length of loosely woven gauze strip. The *kameez* is a similarly loose-fitting long shirt, traditionally with a mandarin collar, but more and more frequently in our modern times with a western-style collar. There is a slit along the side seam on either side and both the front and the rear panel are somewhat rounded.

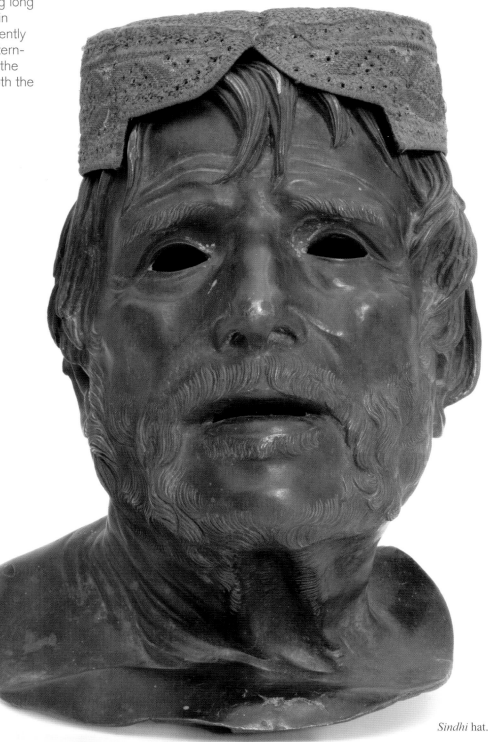

Sindhi hat.

137

Kufi hat.

Turbans are frequently tied around a *Patkha* or *Kulla*, namely a dome-shaped hard cap with fine embroidery. However, in the tribal areas along the Afghan-Pakistani border, long strips of loosely woven turban cloth may be tied directly around the wearer's head, just like in these two photos.

Black *lungee* (turban), twenty-four-feet long, in very fine weave turban cloth.

White *lungee* (turban), twenty-four-feet long, thick turban cloth.

A pair of locally made plastic slippers.

39. ARMY SAPPER IN KZS CAMOUFLAGE UNIFORM

SSh60 steel helmet worn over peaked field cap with earflaps, sapper's tool kit, *private-purchase* rucksack.

SSh60 steel helmet worn over peaked field cap with earflaps, helmet liner string must be loosened to accommodate the field cap with the folded earflaps.

POMZ-2 Anti-Personnel, fragmentation stake mine with a MUV pull fuse. The safety pin and the safety sleeve have been removed, the striker retaining pin is clearly visible.

Sapper's kit with demolition tools and explosive ordnance disposal equipment in three hardened canvas-covered boxes strung on a canvas-webbing belt.

Two of these crated and unused POMZ-2 mines with MUV fuses were found in an abandoned industrial building north of Pul-e Khumri, Baghlan Province in early 2011. Both were demilled on the spot. POMZ mines were normally used in pairs, or small clusters, and they were linked to tripwires.

Sapper's kit, close-up view of contents, pliers are carried in a pouch on the inner side of the middle box lid, a spool of trip wire is clearly visible next to a set of snap hooks, safety pins, and brass safety sleeves for MUV fuses on a green canvas board.

40. KZS CAMOUFLAGE UNIFORMS

Made from different loose-weave cotton fabrics in different colors,
and PFM-1 and PMN-2 mines.

KZS camo jackets made from two highly different fabrics in different colors, (detail), close-up of manufacturer's date and size stamps (1974 and 87) on sewn-in labels.

KZS camo trousers made from two highly different fabrics in different colors.

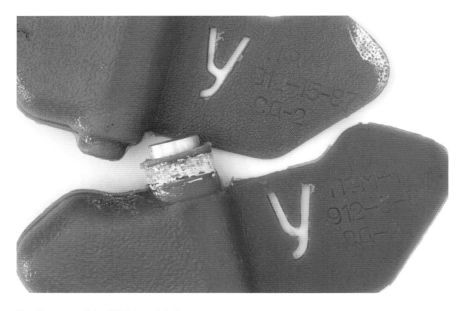

Small, scatterable PFM-1 anti-infantry high-explosive land mines (detail).

The PFM-1 is also known as a butterfly mine, or the "green parrot." The PFM-1 was frequently mistaken for a toy by children, who were destined to pay a terrible price for their mistake. In actual fact, the shape of the PFM-1, which—for all practical purposes—was a plastic container filled with a liquid explosive, was dictated by function and not by any cruel intensions of weapons designers. PFM-1s were deployed en masse in Afghanistan even from low-flying helicopters. These green and brown examples are training versions. The Cyrillic Y (pronunciation "U") stands for *uchebny*, which means "training." The manufacturer's date stamps (87) are clearly visible.

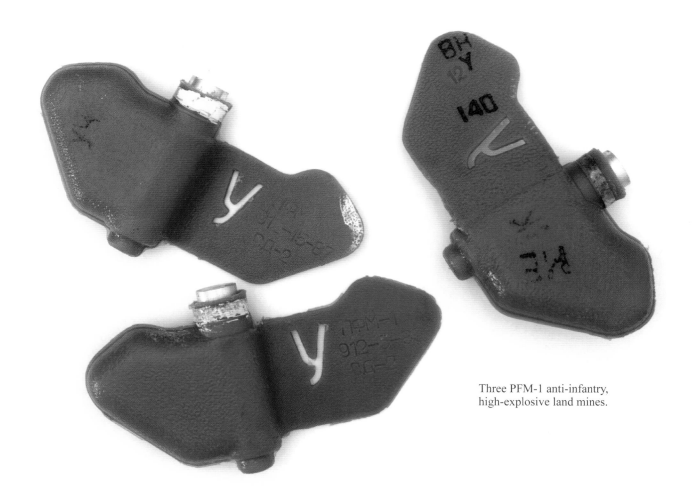

Three PFM-1 anti-infantry, high-explosive land mines.

PMN-2 anti-personnel mine, overhead view. The plastic mine casing is leaf-green, the black rubber X-shaped pressure plate on top and the arming key on the side of the plastic case are clearly visible. The PMN-2 was armed by the rotation and the removal of the arming key.

PMN-2 anti-personnel mine, side view. Manufacturer's date stamp (87) is clearly visible.

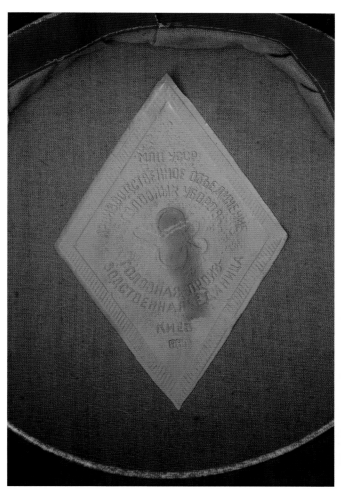

Khaki peaked cap, inside view, (detail), manufacturer's date and size stamp on diamond-shaped simulated leather label (88) is clearly visible.

Single-breasted khaki jacket with the shoulder strap of the "Sam Browne"-type belt under the proporshik shoulder board, NCO (warrant officer) shoulder board with two small stars, Extended Service badge with the number of extra years in service (2) printed on the small brass hanger, two light wound stripes, close-up view.

This *proporshik* (Warrant Officer) wears a single-breasted khaki jacket with a "Sam Browne"-type belt, matching khaki shirt and tie, trousers with red stripes along the outer seams according to his arm of service (Motor Transport), a khaki peaked cap with red color piping and black cap band in proper arm colors, black plastic chin strap, oval NCO cap badge, and black plastic visor as well as high boots.

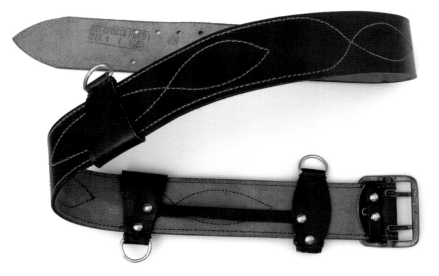

"Sam Browne"-type belt, manufacturer's date and size stamp (88) is clearly visible.

42. SOVIET ARMY PRIVATE

On patrol outside Kabul in the first few days after the invasion of Afghanistan.

EM's winter field jacket with plain collar, matching winter field trousers with padded flannel lining, tucked into the *ryadovoy*'s jackboots. His *ushankah* fur hat bears the enlisted men's enameled red star cap badge with "hammer and sickle" symbol.

AKM/AKS bayonets in scabbard, second pattern (top), early/transitional pattern (bottom).

AKM bayonets drawn from their scabbards, second pattern (top), early/transitional pattern (bottom).

EM's winter field jacket with plain collar, (detail), armored troops' collar badges on subdued/khaki collar tabs and plain shoulder boards of a *ryadovoy*.

EM's winter field jacket, (detail), khaki flannel liner.

EM's winter field jacket, rear view.

43. *GORKA* TWO-PIECE OVERSUIT

Light blue and white striped *Telnyashka* shirt, Chinese-made three-cell chest rig, *Mabuta* hat and Adidas shoes.

The meaning and the etymology of the word *Gorka* is somewhat murky. It is a widely held view that this oversuit derives its name from its originally intended purpose, namely mountain warfare. The *Gorka* two-piece suit, especially the hooded jacket, was so popular with front-line troops that it was extensively used by specialist troops, such as VDV and *Spetsnaz* in Afghanistan.

Gorka jacket with integral hood, (detail), concealed buttons are clearly visible.

Gorka trousers, (detail), suspenders attached with buttons, cargo pockets with button closure on both sides, button fly open, front view.

Gorka trousers, (detail), legs with the unique Gorka design of sewn-in elastic bands are clearly visible.

Gorka two-piece oversuit, light blue and white striped telnyashka shirt, Chinese-made three-cell chest rig with red and green signal flares and a forty-round AKM/RPK47 magazine.

44. AIR FORCE LIEUTENANT IN LIGHT SUMMER EVERYDAY UNIFORM

Comprising a *Pilotka* cap with blue piping, a short waist cropped jacket with matching khaki shirt and tie, breeches with blue stripes along the outer seams according to his service arm (air force), and high boots.

Breeches with blue stripes along the outer seams, (detail), close-up of button fly and metal hook, as almost always on Soviet uniform trousers.

Air Force lieutenant's short, waist cropped jacket with shoulder board, (detail).

Pilotka cap with blue piping and air force officer's cap badge.

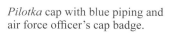

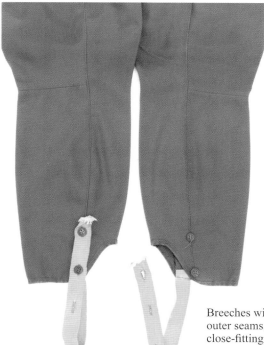

Breeches with blue stripes along the outer seams, (detail), close-up of close-fitting lower section from knees to ankles with Soviet standard adjustable webbing heel loops.

157

45. AIRBORNE/VDV/OFFICER IN COVERALLS

Jumpsuit without rank insignia, "Sam Browne"-type belt with
Makarov pistol holster, officer's field service peaked hat, as well
as fine, leather high boots.

Airborne/VDV/coveralls, jumpsuit, (detail), without rank insignia, "parachute with two aircraft" airborne pin badges on collars without collar tabs are clearly visible.

Airborne/VDV/coveralls, jumpsuit, (detail), rear view, convenient "drop seat" design with wide opening along the waistline and buttoned closure.

Airborne/VDV/coveralls, jumpsuit,
(detail), distinctive thigh pocket on
right side and diamond-shape
reinforced knees.

Officer's field service peaked hat
with subdued khaki piping and
matching khaki cap band regardless
of his proper arm colors, a khaki
green plastic chin strap, a subdued
green-painted oval NCO cap badge
and a khaki green plastic visor.

46. AIRBORNE/VDV/TROOPER M88 *AFGANKA* UNIFORM

With *Afganka/Panamka* hat, as well as lace-up boots, and carrying a Soviet-made chest rig and an RD-54 rucksack with attached sleeping bag.

Afganka/Panamka hat with enlisted men's enameled red star cap badge with "hammer and sickle" symbol, side view.

Afganka/Panamka hat with grommet vent holes, rear view.

Lace-up boots with
distinctive sole pattern.

Lace-up boots marked a major improvement in
foot comfort as compared to traditional foot wraps
and army high boots.

Soviet-made chest rig, three large pockets held two AK-74 magazines each, two grenade pockets on either side held a total of four F1 hand grenades.

Soviet-made chest rig, rear view.

Soviet-made chest rig, (detail),
adjustable neck/shoulder strap with
webbing reinforcement, waist strap,
a thirty-round and a forty-five-round
AK-74 magazine in mag pocket and
an F1 hand grenade in each
side-mounted grenade pocket.

Front view with full kit.

RD-54 rucksack harness along with the AKM bayonet, the integral RD-54 two-cell AK magazine pouch, a Makarov pistol holster, the entrenching tool in its tight fitting RD-54 canvas webbing carrier and the integral RD-54 grenade pouch for two F1 hand grenades are visible as they are attached to the standard army belt with brass buckle (viewed from behind a soldier).

Rear side of RD-54 rucksack with full kit.

Front view of RD-54 harness, the rear side of the RD-54 rucksack is visible in the background.

RD54 canvas webbing E-tool carrier and the standard Soviet Army entrenching tool. As compared to an also available folding shovel, the fixed blade heavy-duty Soviet E-tool was much more than a shovel for a *dyesantnik*. Among a million other purposes, it was put to good use on a daily basis as a formidable edged weapon, a survival tool, and a measuring instrument.

The integral RD-54 two-cell AK magazine pouch and the integral RD54 grenade pouch for two F1 hand grenades (detail).

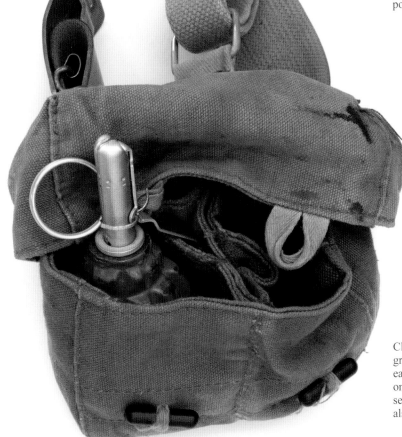

Close-up view of the integral RD-54 grenade pouch with an F1 hand grenade in each pocket. Small internal pockets sewn onto the partition wall were intended for securing the spoon of hand grenades and also for storing spare grenade fuses (detail).

48. AIRBORNE SOLDIER'S/VDV/RD-54 RUCKSACK, AND M88 *AFGANKA* UNIFORM

Rear view with full kit. A rare example of a *Dyesantnik* wearing a blue beret on field duty. A white plastic VDV canteen, as well as a three-piece aluminum VDV canteen are attached to the standard leather belt.

VDV canteen in canvas pouch. The aluminum canteen bottle in this three-piece assembly has a screw cap.

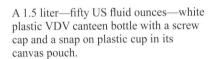

A 1.5 liter—fifty US fluid ounces—white plastic VDV canteen bottle with a screw cap and a snap on plastic cup in its canvas pouch.

White plastic VDV canteen bottle, the screw cap and the snap on plastic cup are clearly visible.

49. SOVIET ARMY HOODED SLEEPING BAG

with white canvas liner and cargo webbing belts.

Hooded sleeping bag, button closure (detail).

The white canvas liner with ribbon closure is placed on top of the sleeping bag.

50. *DHOZD* (RAIN) WATERPROOF RUBBERIZED CANVAS RAIN CAPE/GROUND SHEET

With an inflatable section and inflatable pouch.

The *dhozd* was preferred by Spetsnaz and VDV units to the standard Army-issue *plash-palatka* rain cape/ground sheet, since the green and the white sides *of the dhozd* made it the best conceivable device for camouflaging a soldier lying low in tall grass, or on ice and snow, as the case may be. The *dhozd* had an inflatable section and also a separate inflatable pouch that offered extra warmth in the cold and extra protection against the sharp edges of rocks on the ground.

Dhozd (detail), white side out, drawstring around the pouch, OTK quality control stamp is clearly visible on the white surface near the green edge.

Dhozd (detail). Separately inflatable ribs offered flexibility and greater protection.

51. MUJAHID COMMANDER WEARS A WOODLAND CAMOUFLAGE US M65 JACKET

Sateen *lungee* tied around a dome-shaped hard cap, finely embroidered with silver thread, *shemag* (shawl), Chinese-made chest rig over a *shalwar kameez*, and locally-made leather sandals.

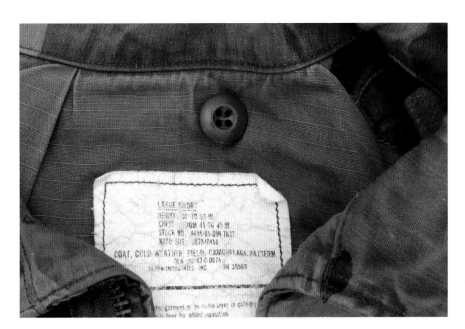

The woodland camouflage US M65 jacket, along with an AKS74U assault rifle with a forty-five-round magazine and the iconic Casio F91 watch with a small compass on the wrist strap, frequently showed up in the posed photographs of an infamous, non-native guerilla leader as well. Collar with label bearing a DLA contract number that suggests the year of manufacture was 1982.

Woodland camouflage US M65 jackets, just like the olive green variant of the same windproof, water-repellent field jacket, were prized items of quite a few Mujahid commanders.

Three different sateen *lungees* are presented along with their original wrapping papers featuring colorful oriental designs, advertising their different manufacturers respectively.

Lungee, the colored, striped sateen material is starched in proper fashion. It is a two piece-wear, since it is tied around a *patkha*, or a *kulla*, namely a dome-shaped hard cap. One end of the *lungee* makes the *shamla*, which looks like the crest of a peacock and the other loose end of the turban cloth, which may be as long as 16-20 feet, forms the tail, that hangs loosely at the back. In less formal situations this dangling piece of turban cloth may be used for wiping the face of its wearer.

Lungee, the *shamla*, and the tail of
the turban, (detail).

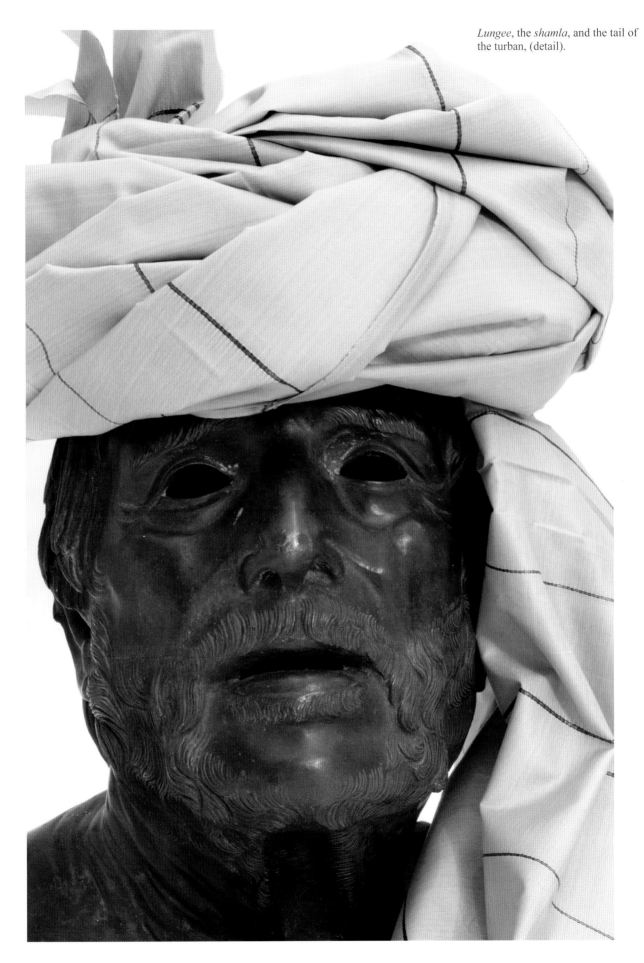

52. MUJAHID COMMANDER'S *SHEMAGH* (SHAWL) AND *SHALWAR KAMEEZ*

The kameez, namely the loose fitting shirt, was a Western-style collar.
In a highly conservative and traditional tribal society, this is the mark
of a man who can afford to adopt the latest fashion trend.

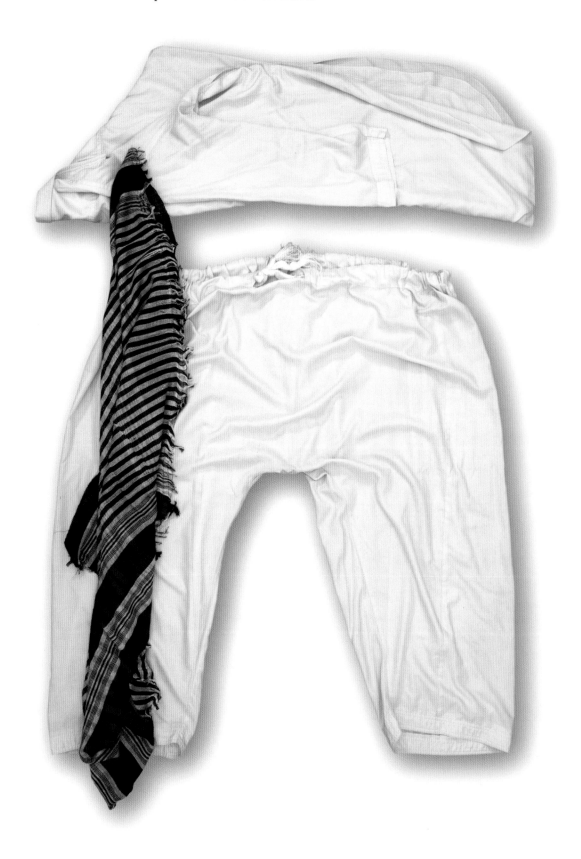

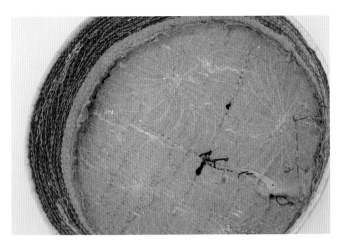

Inside view of the *patkha*, or a *kulla*, namely the dome-shaped hard cap.

Close-up photo of the *patkha*, or a *kulla*, namely the dome-shaped hard cap, which is finely embroidered with silver thread, (detail).

Three *shalwar* trousers, (detail). The cut of each pair of trousers is virtually identical, but they have different colors.

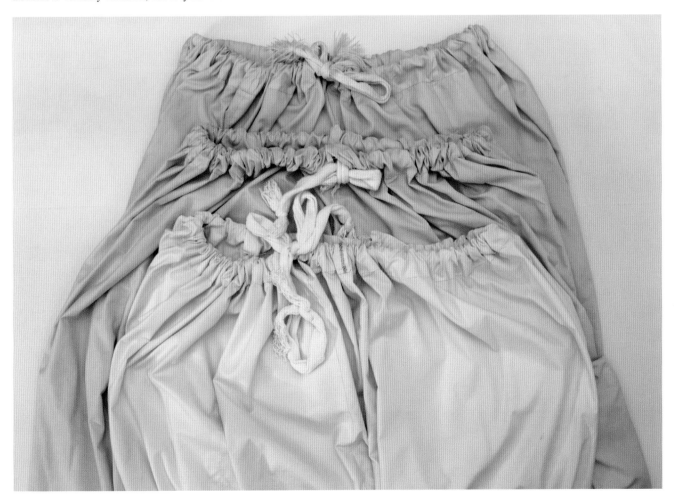

53. *RYADOVOY*, PRIVATE IN A STROYBAT UNIT, M69 FIELD UNIFORM

Featuring a belt with green-painted, steel buckle, khaki peaked cap with red piping and black cap band (in proper service arm colors), black plastic chinstrap, EM's cap badge and black plastic visor, as well as high boots. Also included is a SELGA-405 Transistor Radio.

Army belts. Plain metal belt buckle and painted green buckle. Manufacturer's date (88) and size stamp is clearly visible.

M69 field jacket of a *Ryadovoy*, a private in a STROYBAT, (detail) with a sewn-in collar liner, Army Engineer/ Construction Troops' subdued (green painted) "bulldozer over circular saw, superimposed on anchor and lightning" badge on matching black collar board, *Komsomol* badge on chest.

Komsomol (communist youth
organization) membership card
and badge.

This badge means that the wearer is a *komsomolets*, a
highly disciplined and loyal communist youth. The
membership badge with the image of Lenin and the
abbreviation of the All-Union Leninist Young Communist
League/*VLKSM* in Cyrillic was worn by all young
servicemen in the Soviet armed forces. The military
version of the badge was the screw-back type.

The last entry in the *Komsomol* membership
card is dated May 1987, and identifies its
bearer as a *ryadovoy*; a private in the army.

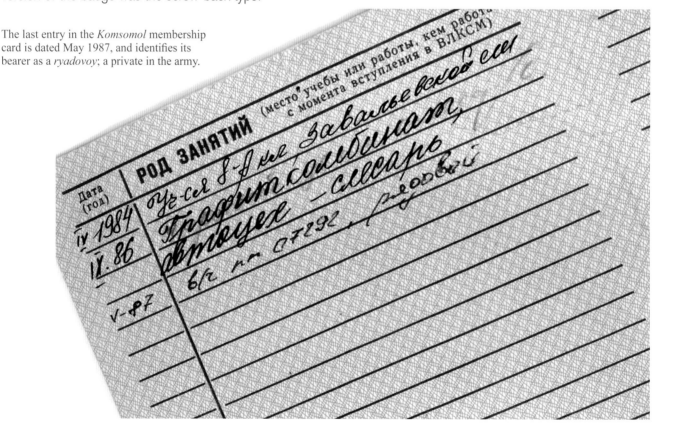

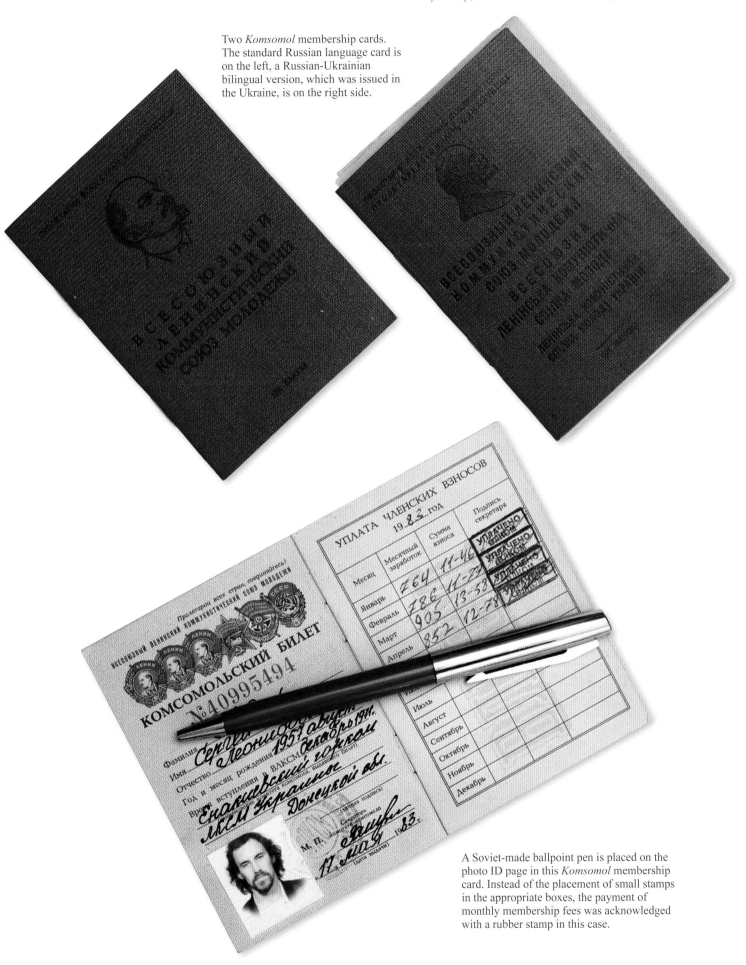

Two *Komsomol* membership cards. The standard Russian language card is on the left, a Russian-Ukrainian bilingual version, which was issued in the Ukraine, is on the right side.

A Soviet-made ballpoint pen is placed on the photo ID page in this *Komsomol* membership card. Instead of the placement of small stamps in the appropriate boxes, the payment of monthly membership fees was acknowledged with a rubber stamp in this case.

54. SENTRY ON A SOVIET OUTPOST IN AFGHANISTAN

With steel helmet over an *Afganka* hat. The tanker's protective vest over the M69 field uniform doubles up as a makeshift ammunition carrier.

SSh68 steel helmet on top of an *Afganka* hat, side view. While the wide brim of the hat was crushed by the helmet chin strap and the soldier's view was somewhat limited in this way, troops with steel helmets on top of *Afganka*, a.k.a. *Panamka*, hats were a common sight during the Afghan war.

Tourniquet (top left) in its original plastic wrap, manufacturer's date stamp (1988) is clearly visible. The Soviet Army tourniquet (bottom left) was a rubber strip with two plastic buttons that could be pressed into any of a series of holes in the pale red rubber band to secure it, when it was wound around a wounded limb. The Soviet rubber band tourniquet—more, or less—could stem the flow of traumatic bleeding. Different manufacturer's specifications and date stamps are visible on the rubberized canvas pouches of sterile first aid field dressings. The rubberized canvas pouch could be inserted into the folding skeleton butt of an AKS-74, or an AKS-74U rifle and the tourniquet could be wound around the metal frame.

SSh68 steel helmet on top of an *Afganka* hat, front view.

55. THE TANKER'S PROTECTIVE VEST

The vest doubles up as a makeshift ammunition carrier.

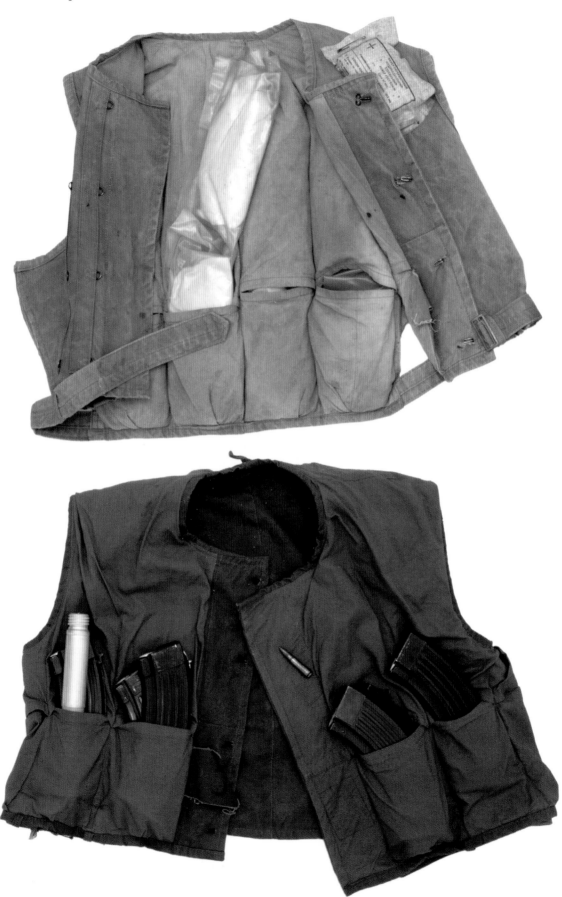

The sterile first aid field dressing in its sealed rubberized canvas pouch is attached to the vest with a safety pin. Cotton wool pads in sealed transparent plastic bags were intended to go into the elongated rectangular inside pockets of the vest, which could give armored crews only a limited measure of protection when they were thrown around inside the metal hull, or when they traveled in the open turret. Mistakenly, the vest is frequently referred to as a buoyancy vest. It testifies to the vast wisdom and unparalleled ingenuity of *tankists* that the obviously useless cotton wool pads were removed and the large pockets were filled with much needed extra AK magazines and signal flares and bayonets, etc. The magazines in the loose pockets were much better protected, if the vest was worn as originally intended, but occasionally the vest was worn inside out.

Tanker's vest without padding, two rows of black-painted loops on one side and matching hooks on the other side were sewn on the heavy-duty canvas material to ensure a tight fit. Plastic and ribbed pressed steel as well as smooth-sided, aka slab-sided thirty-round and forty-round magazines for AK-47 and thirty-round and forty-five-round magazines for AK-74 assault rifles.

Mag pouches, and magazines for Kalashnikov-series weapons (arranged in three columns):

1: a/ forty-round RPK/AK-47 magazine in a four-cell mag pouch with shoulder harness, b/ thirty-round AK-47 magazines in an early-type five-cell mag pouch with shoulder harness, 1st pattern smooth-sided, a.k.a. slab-sided AK-47 magazine.

2: a/ forty-five-round RPK/AK-74 magazine in a four-cell mag pouch with shoulder harness, b/ seventy five-round RPK/ AK-47 drum magazine in belt pouch, c/ thirty-round AK-47 magazines in a three-cell mag pouch with belt loops,

3: a/ thirty-round AK-47 plastic magazine in a three-cell mag pouch with belt loops, b/ thirty-round AK-47 magazines in an four-cell mag pouch with belt loops, c/ thirty-round AK-74 plastic magazine with loader guide and stripper clip holding 5.45x39 mm rounds attached.

56. WOMAN'S M69-STYLE FIELD UNIFORM

Comprising a jacket with subdued field-service shoulder and collar boards, "Goblet with Serpent" medical branch insignia on both collar boards, medical branch sleeve patch on the left sleeve, matching khaki skirt, and high boots.

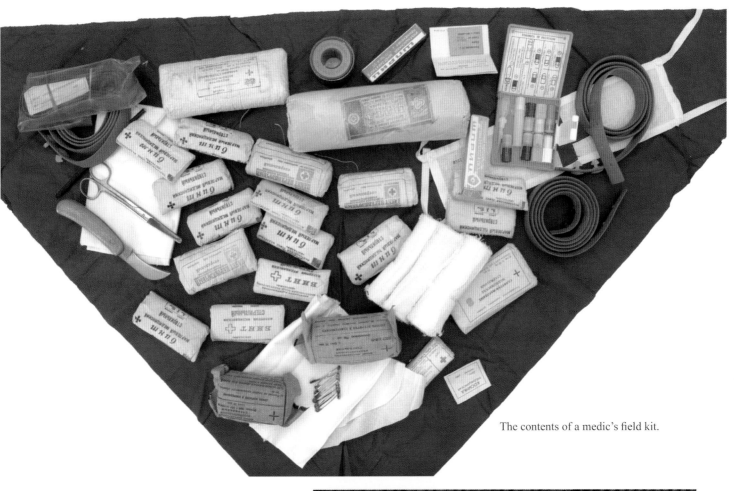

The contents of a medic's field kit.

Outstanding Medic badge.

57. ARMY NURSE, SHIRT SLEEVE ORDER

CA in cyrillic characters (pronunciation "SA") on the shoulder boards stands for "Soviet Army." Soviet army medical service blood pressure gauge.

Soviet Army doctor's blood pressure gauge.
Full set, including plastic pouch.

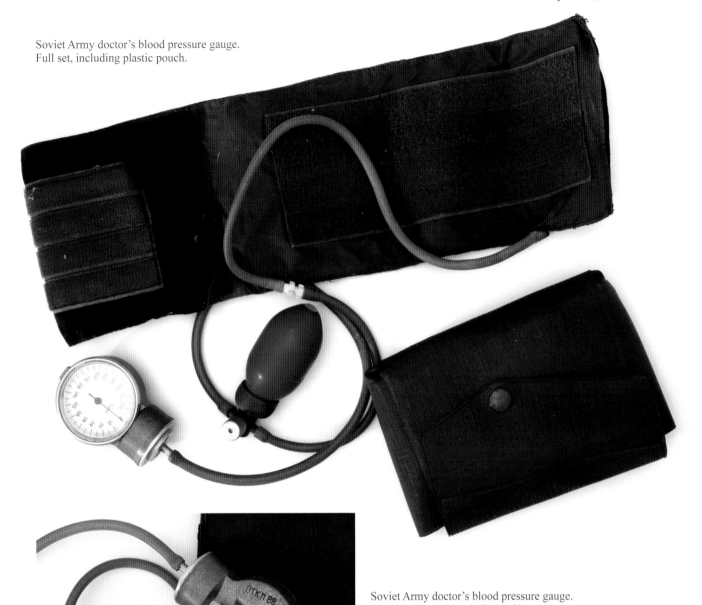

Soviet Army doctor's blood pressure gauge.
(Detail). Blue rubber bulb, bladder, pressure
cuff and rear side of the gauge with OTK
quality acceptance and date (88) stamp.

The sealed, rubberized canvas pouch of a sterile first aid field
dressing is inserted into the folding skeleton butt of an
AKS74U assault rifle. The pale red rubber band tourniquet is
wound around the metal frame and is secured with two plastic
buttons that could be pressed into any of a series of holes in
the rubber band. Since it was the front-line soldiers' invention,
there was no standard way to do it. The important thing was to
keep both the blood stopper and the bandage handy in case of
an emergency, even if the bulging field dressing pouch and the
tourniquet made the docking of the skeleton butt to the
receiver in the folded position quite difficult.

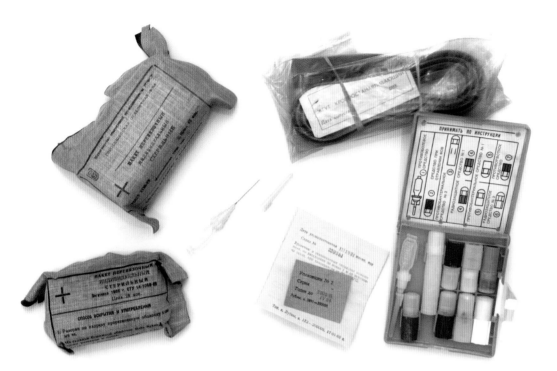

First aid kit of an individual soldier. Two sterile first aid field dressings in sealed rubberized canvas pouches, (left), disposable syringe, painkiller, the most important and practical item in the *Apteka* NBC first aid kit in an orange-color plastic case, (center), tourniquet in its original plastic wrap, manufacturer's date stamp (1988) is clearly visible, (top right), orange-color *Apteka* nuclear-biological-chemical (NBC) warfare first aid kit with instruction sheet, manufacturer's date stamp (1981) and "best before" date (1984) are clearly visible, (bottom right).

Orange-color *Apteka* nuclear-biological-chemical (NBC) warfare first aid kit with   instruction sheet in the lid. Various configurations of this kit existed. While the majority of pills in clearly marked and color-coded plastic tube containers were supposed to treat the casualties of NBC warfare, some items could be utilized in less dramatic scenarios, as well. For example, pills in the small container with a light blue screw cap, which were supposed to stop vomiting, also treated an upset stomach, or a massive hangover. The most important and (only) practical item in the *Apteka* NBC first aid kit was the painkiller, an analgesic drug in a disposable syringe. In spite of the fact that this kit is shown in Soviet war footage, a 1988 Soviet film set in Afghanistan, and also in one of the most dramatic scenes in a world-famous Afghan war movie that was made in Russia more than fifteen years after the Soviet withdrawal from Afghanistan, the orange-color *Apteka* kit was not general issue to Soviet troops. Its limited use may be attributable to the fact that the painkiller was a potent drug, which was very much in demand among troops who would otherwise use locally made hash, or other similarly illegal substances.

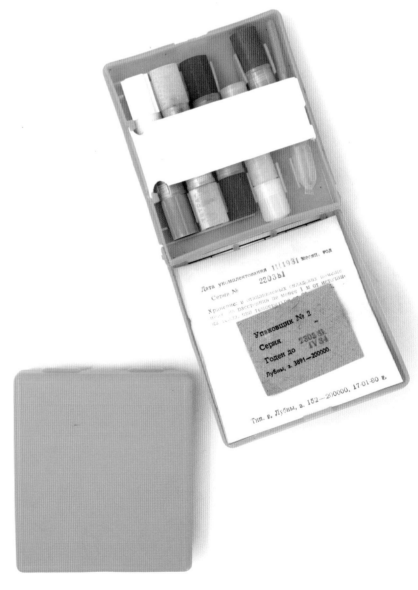

Envelope of a letter home from a soldier in
Afghanistan with military postal stamps on both
sides. The envelope shows an army medic
treating a wounded soldier and celebrates the
fortieth anniversary of WWII.

58. ARMY NURSE IN M88 *AFGANKA* SUMMER FIELD UNIFORM

Ankle boots and a peaked field service cap with earflaps, bearing an EM's subdued (painted green) cap badge, and army medic's bag.

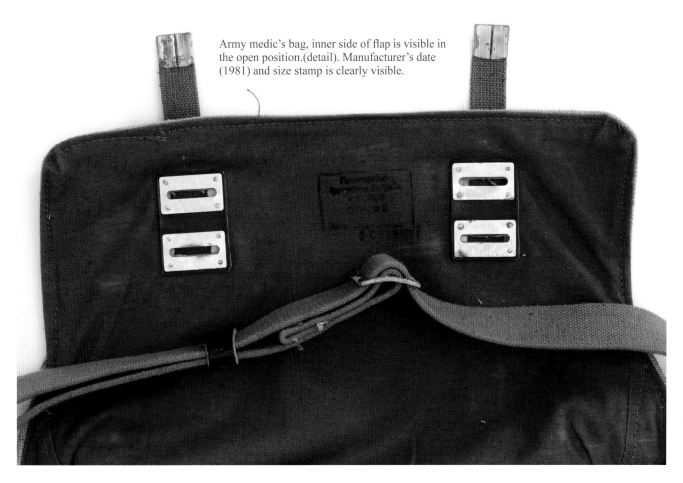

Army medic's bag, inner side of flap is visible in the open position.(detail). Manufacturer's date (1981) and size stamp is clearly visible.

Army medic's bag. Closed flap with Red Cross symbol in white circle, front view. The shoulder webbing strap and the webbing waist strap are clearly visible.

59. EM'S OLIVE GREEN IMPREGNATED, WATERPROOF *PLASH-PALATKA* RAIN CAPE/GROUND SHEET

Worn over an M88 *Afganka* winter field uniform.

One corner of the rain cape may be fashioned into a hood by pulling both ends of a draw string that runs between the *plash-palatka* and a strip of the same canvas material that was sewn on in a semi circular pattern. The front of the EM's *plash-palatka* poncho may be closed with five wooden-pegs on one side and matching leather grommets on the other side. A soldier may push one arm through a large slot on the right-hand side of a closed *plash-palatka*, which, however, was typically worn unbuttoned.

Full kit comprising a plash-palatka rain cape–ground sheet (shelter half), a two-piece tent pole, tent stakes, and a tent rope. The plash-palatka is fashioned into a poncho, a hood is formed with the attached draw strings, one rear corner is folded up and is secured with a wooden peg.

60. MOTORIZED RIFLE LIEUTENANT'S DOUBLE-BREASTED STEEL-GREY GREATCOAT

"Sam Browne"-type belt, "everyday" service khaki peaked cap, high boots.

Motorized rifle officer's "everyday" service khaki peaked cap with oval officer's cockade, red piping and red hat band in proper arm colors of motorized rifle troops, gilt chin strap, and black plastic visor.

"Sam Browne"-type belt. Manufacturer's specifications and date stamp (1986) is clearly visible.

Motorized Rifle Lieutenant's double-breasted steel-grey greatcoat with larger size, "greatcoat style" shoulder board, "five-pointed star surrounded by two oak leaf branches" badge on red collar board, which is the proper arm color of motorized rifle troops (detail).

61. THE M88 *AFGANKA* WINTER FIELD UNIFORM

Worn by a Soviet NCO at the homecoming parade at Termez, Uzbekistan, on February 15, 1989, with the medal to commemorate the "10th Anniversary of the Saur Revolution," as well as the medal "From the Grateful Afghan People."

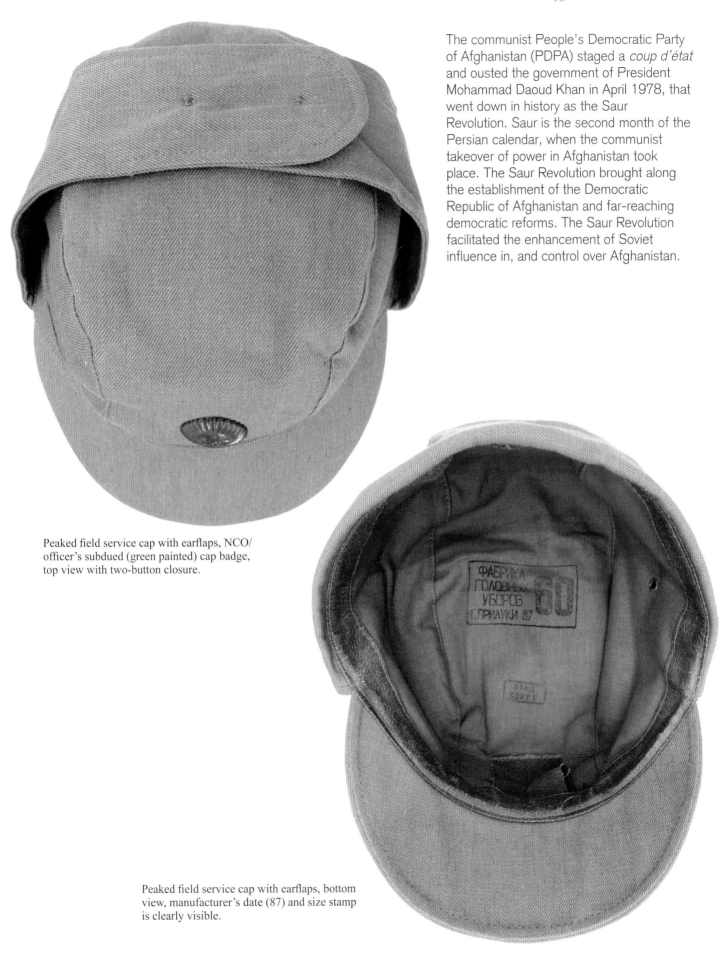

The communist People's Democratic Party of Afghanistan (PDPA) staged a *coup d'état* and ousted the government of President Mohammad Daoud Khan in April 1978, that went down in history as the Saur Revolution. Saur is the second month of the Persian calendar, when the communist takeover of power in Afghanistan took place. The Saur Revolution brought along the establishment of the Democratic Republic of Afghanistan and far-reaching democratic reforms. The Saur Revolution facilitated the enhancement of Soviet influence in, and control over Afghanistan.

Peaked field service cap with earflaps, NCO/ officer's subdued (green painted) cap badge, top view with two-button closure.

Peaked field service cap with earflaps, bottom view, manufacturer's date (87) and size stamp is clearly visible.

M88 *Afganka* winter field uniform jacket with button-in liner and artificial fur collar. The integral Makarov pistol holster as well as the manufacturer's date (1988) and size stamp are clearly visible.

Rear view of the medal issued by the Democratic Republic of Afghanistan to commemorate the "10th Anniversary of the Saur Revolution."

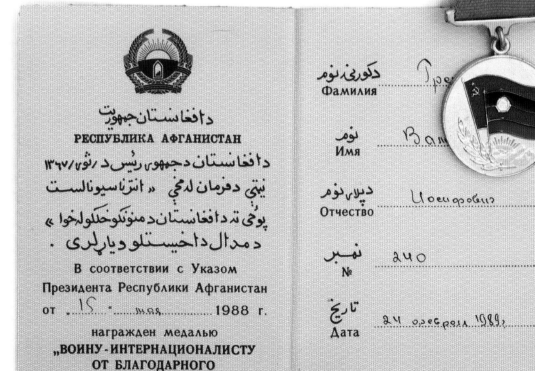

Medal "From the Grateful Afghan People" with matching award document. This Afghan medal was awarded by the Najibullah government of the Democratic Republic of Afghanistan to departing Soviet soldiers for outstanding military service in Afghanistan. The Soviet and Afghan flags adorn the front side. The wording on the back says "From the Grateful Afghan People."

62. THE M69 FIELD UNIFORM WITH MEDALS AND BADGES

Worn by a Soviet junior sergeant at the homecoming parade at Termez, Uzbekistan, on February 15, 1989. A *Telnyashka* t-shirt is worn along with an EM grade *Ushankah* hat with EM cap badge, and high boots.

M69 field uniform with medals and badges.

M69 Field Uniform.
Top row: Army EM's Qualifications Badge, Grade 3, Outstanding Soldier badge, Guard Unit badge.
Bottom row: Soldier-Sportsman badge, Grade I, Parachutist Badge, two jumps.

M69 field uniform, (detail bottom left), subdued khaki field shoulder board with two narrow red ribbons, denoting junior sergeant, "parachute with two aircraft" airborne pin badge on subdued khaki field collar board.

M69 field uniform, (detail, bottom right), Jubilee medal "70 Years of the Armed Forces of the USSR," medal issued by the Democratic Republic of Afghanistan to commemorate the "10th Anniversary of the Saur Revolution" (front side) as well as the medal "From the Grateful Afghan People," *Komsomol* badge (lower center).

Turkestan Military District (TurkVO) badge
on M69 jacket.

Soviet Army belt, resin coated canvas webbing belt with
"red star with hammer and sickle" symbol on brass buckle,
manufacturer's date (88) and size stamp on rear side of belt
is clearly visible. Soldiers referred to it as *derevany* because
of its stiffness. Officers, in general, wore leather belts and
most soldiers after the completion of their first year in
service reached a point in their military career where they
could buy a leather belt in a Voenntorg military store, which
operated in almost each military garrison.

The Turkestan Military District (*Turkestansky
voyeny okrug*) was one of the military districts of
the Soviet armed forces. Among a number of
other units and military organizations, the 40th
Army in Kabul, one VDV airborne division, and
eight motor rifle divisions belonged to the
TurkVO's area of responsibility and served under
Turkestan Military District command.

The final chapter in the movie *9th Company*,
directed by Fedor Bondarchuk, about the heroism
displayed by Soviet troops in defending Hill 3234
against a series of attacks by a large group of
Mujahideen warriors is *loosely* based on an
incident involving the "9th Company," 345th
Independent Guards Airborne Regiment, 103rd
Guards Airborne Division, a subordinated unit of
the Turkestan Military District.

63. MUJAHID COMMANDER

Near Torabora, Nangarhar Province in eastern Afghanistan in the early phase of the war, this commander wears a *Shalwar Kameez*, knitted wool sweater, *Pakol* hat, leather sandals and a *Patoo* (a thick shawl), on the right shoulder.

Two different types of *patoo*. The thick wool shawl on top is made of much finer wool and is machine embroidered at both ends. The *patoo* below is a common type. *Patoos* like this are worn in cold weather by a lot of Afghans, especially in rural areas. An ordinary patoo would have this quality and color, machine embroidered white stripes with a geometric patterns at either end as well as green stripes along the edges.

The *Pakol* is a traditional round hat made of pure wool. Sewn-in ribs in single, double, or triple rows along the sides serve as an ornament and also give the hat a measure of stiffness, when the sides are neatly rolled up into a band almost all the way to the flat top panel. In a similarly authentic, although less frequent configuration the sides are folded up into a flat band around the head.

Pakol hats in different colors.

64. *SPETSODEZHDA* TWO-COLOR STAIR STEP CAMOUFLAGE PATTERN SUMMER UNIFORM OF KGB BORDER GUARD ENLISTED PERSONNEL

With bright green peaked cap with red color piping and dark blue cap band, black plastic chinstrap, "Wreathed Red Star" EM's cap badge and black plastic visor, and high boots.

Spetsodezhda two-color stair step camouflage pattern summer uniform jacket, 2nd pattern, the cut is identical to that of the M88 *Afganka* summer uniform jacket. No attempt was made to restore this jacket and it is presented here exactly as it was purchased in Termez, Uzbekistan.

65. *SPETSODEZHDA* TWO-COLOR STAIR STEP CAMOUFLAGE PATTERN WINTER UNIFORM, SECOND PATTERN

The cut is identical to that of the M88 *Afganka* winter uniform. Primarily worn by KGB border guard personnel.

Spetsodezhda two color stair step camouflage pattern winter uniform, second pattern, side view of jacket, integral Makarov pistol holster and string lanyard on the left-hand side are clearly visible.

Spetsodezhda Two-color Stair Step Camouflage Pattern Winter Uniform, Second Pattern

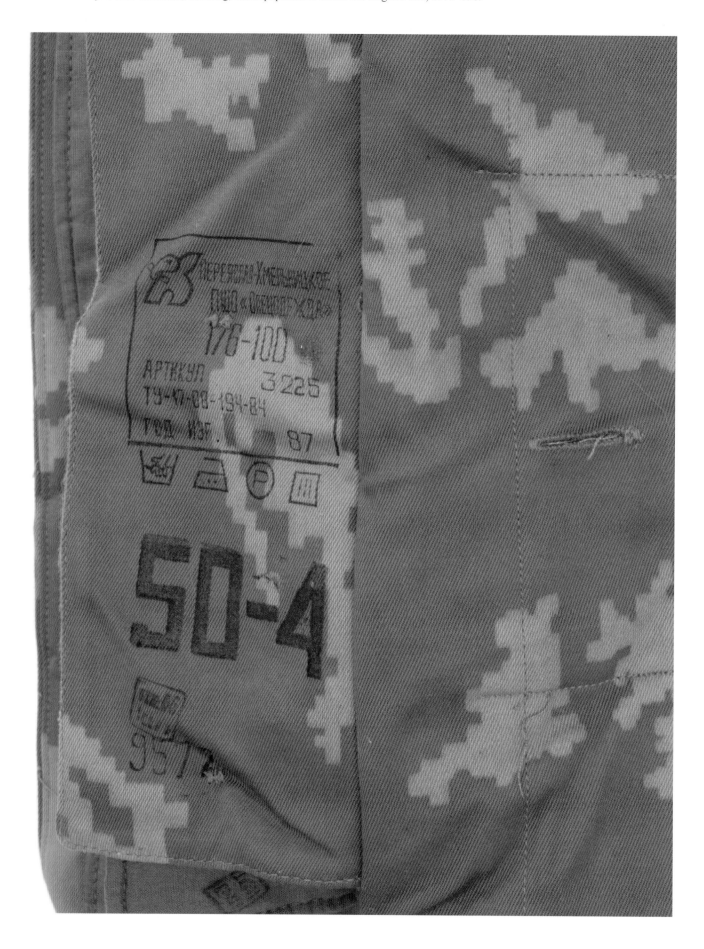

Spetsodezhda two-color stair step camouflage pattern peaked field service cap with earflaps, no cap badge is attached (front view).

Spetsodezhda two-color stair step camouflage pattern peaked field service cap with earflaps (inside view), manufacturer's date (88) and size stamp as well as grey simulated leather sweat band are clearly visible.

66. M69 PATTERN SUMMER FIELD UNIFORM OF A BORDER GUARD SERGEANT WITH DECORATIONS AND BADGES

Worn even on field duty with a bright green peaked cap with red color piping and dark blue cap band, black plastic chinstrap, "Wreathed Red Star" cap badge and black plastic visor, and high boots.

M69 pattern summer field uniform of a Border Guard
sergeant, sewn-in collar liner, sergeant's "border guard"
green shoulder boards and "five-pointed star surrounded
by two oak leaf branches" badges on green collar
boards, which is the proper service color of KGB
Border Guard troops. (detail).

Leather belt with "red star with hammer and
sickle" symbol on brass buckle, manufacturer's
date (1977) and size stamp on rear side of belt.

M69 pattern summer field uniform of a Border Guard sergeant with decorations and badges (detail):

Left/Top: "suspended star"-type badge, "Outstanding Border Guard," 1st Class.
Middle row: Army EM's Qualifications Badge, Grade 3, Commander/Senior ranking member of a Border Guard patrol badge, Outstanding Soldier badge.
Bottom row: Soldier-Sportsman badge, Grade II.
Right: "60 Years of Border Guard Service" jubilee badge, Komsomol badge.

M69 pattern summer field uniform of a Border Guard sergeant, sewn-in collar liner with OTK and size stamp (detail). Linen undercollars were either folded strips of fabric and were ironed by individual soldiers, who also had to sew them in, or they were mass produced items and could be purchased in the local Voenntorg military store, like this one.

67. LONG, DARK BROWNISH-GREY GREATCOAT OF KGB BORDER GUARD ENLISTED PERSONNEL

Worn with a bright green peaked cap with red color piping and dark blue cap band, black plastic chinstrap, "Wreathed Red Star" EM's cap badge, and black plastic visor, and high boots.

The *ПВ* Cyrillic characters (pronunciation "PV") on the oversized "greatcoat-style" green shoulder boards stand for "Border Guard;" "five-pointed star surrounded by two oak leaf branches" badges are displayed on green collar boards, which is the proper service color of KGB Border Guard troops. The KGB Border Guard service sleeve patch is displayed on the left arm of the overcoat (detail).

Although the greatcoat may be closed with metal hooks and loops that are mounted on the opposite sides of the front on reinforced circular patches made of the same heavy-duty material, a single column of five buttons is displayed on the front for decoration, only.

KGB Border Guard enlisted personnel's/sergeant's bright green peaked cap with red color piping and dark blue cap band, black plastic chin strap, "wreathed red star" EM's cap badge, and black plastic visor.

KGB Border Guard officer's bright green peaked cap with red color piping and dark blue cap band, gilt chin strap, officer's parade cap badge and black plastic visor.

Postcard featuring a Border Guard dog handler with his K9 companion on a leash. The Border Guard is wearing a field service winter jacket with an artificial fur collar, matching winter trousers, and high boots.

Front page of the DOSAAF service dog pedigree with small DOSAAF enameled badge, Stud Dog qualification tag (aluminum with green lacquer) and Service Dog Qualification Badge, 1st Class (aluminum with inscriptions in red).

Posed propaganda photograph of KGB Border Guard dog handlers on field duty, wearing M69 field service uniforms, carrying light combat load.

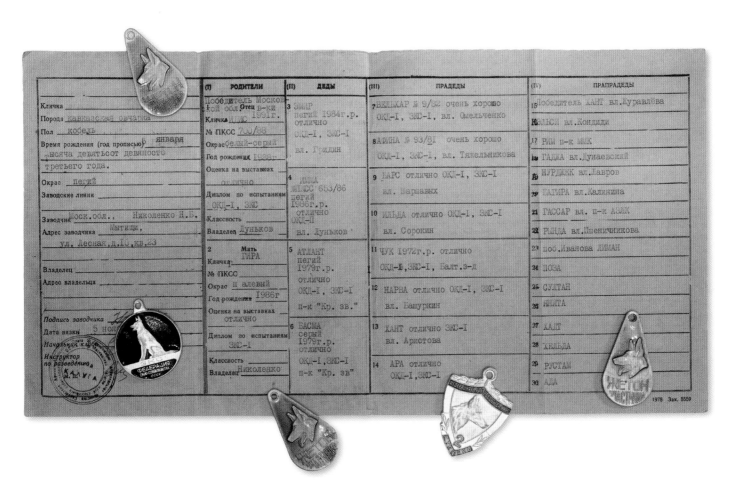

KGB Border Guard service dog's pedigree with detailed identification information of four generations of the dog's forebears. The qualification badges of this particular male purebred Caucasian *Ovtcharka*, i.e. shepherd dog, are also displayed on the pedigree. The pedigree chart is clearly visible in the document that was issued and duly kept by the Volunteer Society for Cooperation with the Army, Aviation, and Fleet (DOSAAF), namely a paramilitary sport organization in the USSR. Service dogs for the Soviet armed forces were bred and trained and qualified under the auspices of DOSAAF. In a similar fashion, qualification badges were awarded by DOSAAF.

68. KGB BORDER GUARD *DEMBEL*'S CUSTOMIZED UNIFORM AT THE END OF HIS TOUR IN AFGHANISTAN

KGB border guard enlisted personnel's bright green peaked cap, single-breasted EM grade khaki jacket with matching khaki shirt and tie, EM grade khaki trousers without service-color stripes along the outer seams, and high boots.

KGB Border Guard green sleeve patch, *dembel*'s customized version with junior officer's rank star mounted on top of the printed "five-pointed star surrounded by two oak leaf branches" on the patch.

KGB Border Guard single-breasted EM's-grade khaki jacket with decorations and badges:

Left top row – Leningrad KGB Border Guard Unit.
Second row – "Outstanding Border Guard," 2nd Class, "Outstanding Border Guard," 1st Class.
Third row – Army EM's Qualifications Badge, Grade 3, Commander/Senior ranking member of a Border Guard patrol badge, Outstanding Soldier badge.
Fourth row – *Razryad* Sports Qualifications Badge in Track and Field, 2nd Class, Soldier-Sportsman badge, Grade II.
Bottom row – *Razryad* Sports Qualifications Badge in Motorsport/Aviation, 2nd Class. *Razryad* means qualification grade in Russian, and each *Razryad* badge shows a pictogram of the relevant sport as well as the ranking, or qualification grade of the wearer of the badge.

Right top row – Medal "For Distinction in Guarding the State Border of the USSR," Jubilee medal "70 Years of the Armed Forces of the USSR," "From the Grateful Afghan People" medal.
Bottom row – *Komsomol* badge.

KGB Border Guard green shoulder board, *dembel*'s customized version embossed with heavy-gauge brass cutouts of the Cyrillic characters ПВ (pronunciation "PV"), which stand for "Border Guard."

231

Necktie with tie clip. Banded, pre-tied necktie with a permanently attached collar band as well as a hook and eye to secure it around the wearer's neck.

Service-issue tie clip with embossed five-pointed star.

KGB Border Guard green shoulder board for shirt with "five-pointed star, surrounded by two oak leaf branches" badge, *dembel's* customized version, embossed with heavy-gauge brass cutouts of the Cyrillic characters ПВ (pronunciation "PV") that stands for "Border Guard" (top and bottom views).

70. SUMMER WORK DRESS OF A WORKMAN IN A STROYBAT MILITARY CONSTRUCTION DETACHMENT

Telnyashka t-shirt, *Pilotka* cap with EM's enameled red star cap badge, with "Hammer and Sickle" symbol, and high boots.

Work jacket with straight cut hip pockets on either side,
worn outside the matching work trousers.

The work trousers have two straight cut hip pockets and knee reinforcements. They may be worn either outside, or tucked into the high boots.

An assortment of high boots, including officers' genuine
leather boots and EMs' artificial leather *Kirza* boots.

An assortment of high boots with different rubber, plastic
and leather soles and different sole tread groove patterns.

71. *MABUTA* SUMMER FIELD UNIFORM

Telnyashka t-shirt, *Mabuta* peaked field service cap with earflaps, Soviet-made chest rig loaded with AK magazines and hand grenades. One grenade pocket holds a sealed pouch of Chinese-made first-aid bandages.

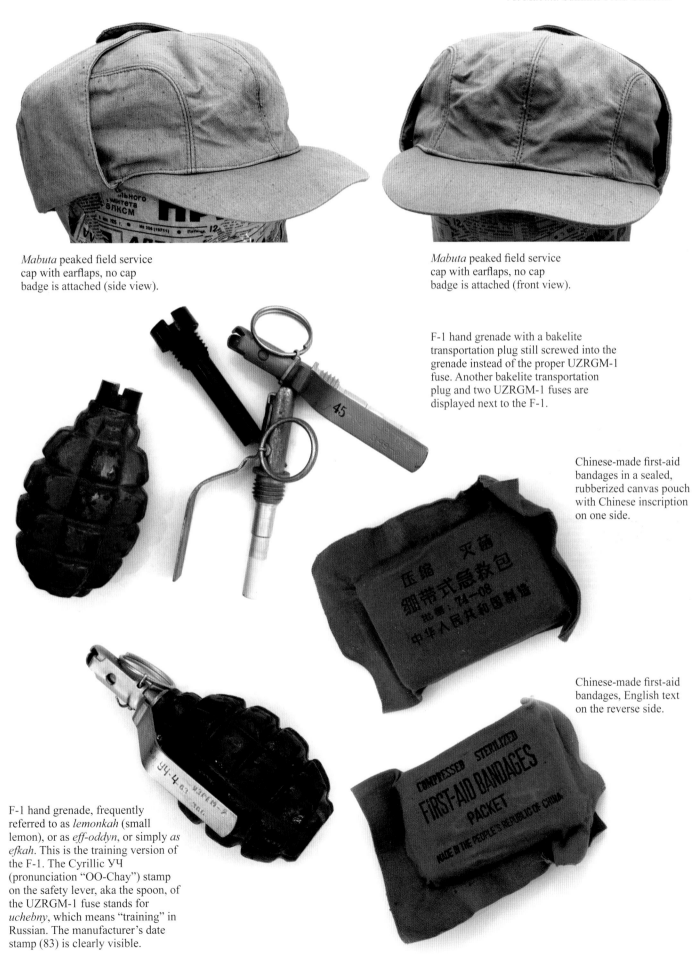

Mabuta peaked field service cap with earflaps, no cap badge is attached (side view).

Mabuta peaked field service cap with earflaps, no cap badge is attached (front view).

F-1 hand grenade with a bakelite transportation plug still screwed into the grenade instead of the proper UZRGM-1 fuse. Another bakelite transportation plug and two UZRGM-1 fuses are displayed next to the F-1.

Chinese-made first-aid bandages in a sealed, rubberized canvas pouch with Chinese inscription on one side.

Chinese-made first-aid bandages, English text on the reverse side.

F-1 hand grenade, frequently referred to as *lemonkah* (small lemon), or as *eff-oddyn*, or simply *as efkah*. This is the training version of the F-1. The Cyrillic УЧ (pronunciation "OO-Chay") stamp on the safety lever, aka the spoon, of the UZRGM-1 fuse stands for *uchebny*, which means "training" in Russian. The manufacturer's date stamp (83) is clearly visible.

Mabuta summer field uniform, trousers, distinctive thigh cargo pockets on either side with double button closure, knife pocket, a unique feature of *Mabuta* summer and winter trousers, on the right-hand side, (detail).

Mabuta summer field uniform trousers, the service boots are tucked under the unique flap on the lower leg section.

Mabuta peaked field service cap with earflaps (detail).

Mabuta summer field uniform jacket. Lightweight khaki canvas material with a mesh insert under the arms. The *Mabuta* uniform was designed to be comfortable in Africa, in tropical rain forests and in scorching desert heat alike. The armpit vents allowed for maximum airflow and were supposed to keep soldiers less sweaty. The short, waist cropped jacket had an elastic band in the waist line that is permanently attached at one end and which goes around the back to the right side and ends in a tab with a buttonhole. Also, the jacket has two adjusting buttons on the inner right side.

72. *MABUTA* WINTER FIELD UNIFORM – TROUSERS, KNITWEAR

The official designation of this uniform was "Winter Jump Suit For Special Operations Troops." *Mabuta* winter trousers, knitted wool cap, knitted wool sweater, and lace-up boots.

In collectors' circles this uniform is named after Mobutu Sese Seko Kuku Ngbendu wa Za Banga, the president of the Democratic Republic of the Congo, that Mobutu himself renamed Zaire. In 1960, Mobutu staged a coup and grabbed power from Prime Minister Lumumba who had received economic assistance and military aid as well as a contingent of over a thousand "technical advisers" from the Soviet Union. Mobutu made short shrift of Lumumba and his Soviet advisers. The prime minister was executed, and all Soviet personnel were expelled from the Congo.

Mobutu, who went down in history as the archetypal African dictator, was notorious for his human rights violations, widespread corruption and nepotism in Zaire, and his embezzlement of billions of US dollars.

Nevertheless, summer and winter variants of this unique type uniform—said to have been designed for Soviet servicemen slated to perform their internationalist duties in Africa—will preserve Mobutu's name.

Knitted wool cap.

Knitted wool five-finger gloves.

Knitted wool balaclava hood. The balaclava hood on the left is displayed inside out to reveal the integral earflaps for extreme cold weather conditions. The balaclava hood on the right could be used as a face mask in extreme cold weather, it could be tucked under the collar of the winter jacket, or the sides could be folded up to form a cap.

Knitted wool sweaters. The close-fitting, round, and high collar and the wrist of the sweater on the left side are displayed in full length, the neck and the cuffs of the sweater on the right-hand side are folded over as if they were actually worn by a soldier in the field.

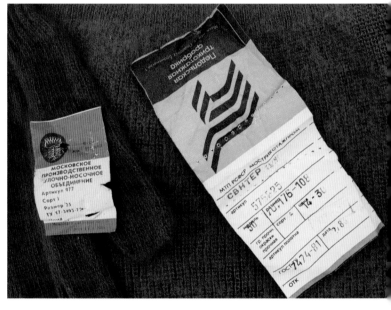

Original manufacturer's labels were sewn onto knitted items. These ones came along with a pair of unissued knitted wool five-finger gloves (left) and a knitted wool sweater (right) from the arsenal of a small Soviet garrison.

Mabuta winter trousers, lower leg (detail), adjusting buttons on both cuffs, lace-up boots.

Mabuta winter trousers, thigh cargo pockets on either side with double button closure, knife pocket, a unique feature of Mabuta summer and winter trousers, is clearly visible on the right-hand side (detail).

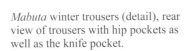

Mabuta winter trousers (detail), rear view of trousers with hip pockets as well as the knife pocket.

73. *MABUTA* WINTER FIELD UNIFORM JACKET

With button-in liner and officer's grade artificial fur collar, matching officer's grade *Ushankah* hat. This VDV officer wears a Chinese-made chest rig, and an M88 *Afganka* field jacket under his *Mabuta* winter jacket.

Rear view of *Mabuta* winter field uniform jacket with button-in liner and officer's grade artificial fur collar as well as the matching officer's grade *ushankah* hat. The button closure on the left cuff, under which a soldier could stow his wrist compass, or a map, or much-needed documents, is clearly visible.

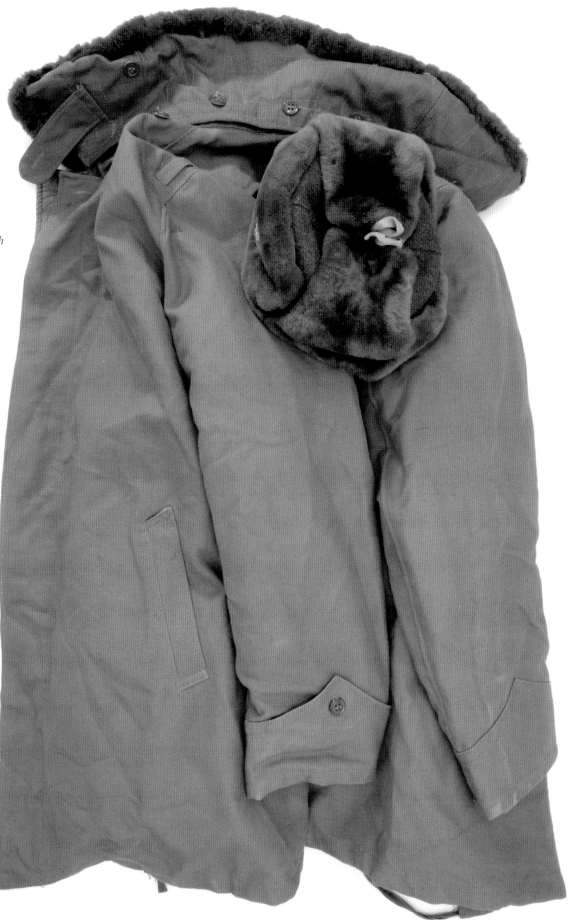

Officer's grade *ushankah* hat made
of much finer quality artificial fur
with air force officer's cap badge.

Collar of M88 *Afganka* field jacket with sewn-in undercollar and "parachute with two aircraft" Airborne pin badges on both sides.

74. ARTILLERY SERGEANT *DEMBEL'S* CUSTOMIZED UNIFORM AT THE END OF HIS TOUR IN AFGHANISTAN

EM's khaki peaked cap, single-breasted EM grade khaki jacket, custom-made aiguillette with an ornamental brass needle, matching khaki shirt and tie, white parade belt with brass buckle. The trousers are EM grade khaki without service-color stripes along the outer seams. High boots.

Artillery sergeant *dembel's* khaki peaked cap with red color piping and black cap band in proper arm colors, black plastic chin strap, EM's "wreathed red star" cap badge, and black plastic visor.

Artillery sleeve patch with superimposed "crossed gun barrels" badge (upside down) on the printed yellow "crossed gun barrels" insignia.

Single-breasted EM's-grade khaki jacket with badges (detail): Outstanding Soldier badge, Army EM's Qualifications Badge, Grade 3, Guard Unit badge, customized shoulder board made of black velvet mounted on a slightly curved plastic plate, sergeant's three stripes made from golden ribbons set against a red background, instead of plain yellow ribbons mounted on a black felt shoulder board, the embossed CA letters in Cyrillic characters (pronunciation "SA") stand for Soviet Army (*Sovyetskaya Armiyah*). Standard black felt collar board with the artillery's "crossed gun barrels" badge, custom-made aiguillette with an ornamental brass needle, matching khaki shirt and tie.

251

75. *RYADOVOY*, PRIVATE IN A MOTOR TRANSPORT UNIT, CUSTOMIZED *DEMBEL* OUTFIT, SHIRT SLEEVE ORDER

Army private's khaki shirt and tie, M69 uniform breeches, khaki peaked cap with red piping and black cap band (in proper service arm colors), black plastic chinstrap, EM's "Wreathed Red Star" cap badge and black plastic visor, and high boots.

Dedovshchina (grandfatherism) meant the uncontrolled power of senior enlisted personnel over young conscripts. *Dedovshchina* was the informal system of the subordination, verbal and physical abuse, and humiliation of virtually all junior conscripts in the Soviet armed forces.

In Soviet army slang, the Russian word *ded*, which literally means granddad, or grandfather, refers to enlisted personnel in their final phase of their conscript service. These all-powerful old boys claimed to have an unalienable right to control and abuse their junior comrades in every conceivable way up until the sacred moment of their honorable discharge from their mandatory conscript service, namely their demobilization. Consequently, the word *dembel*, which means a Soviet conscript to be discharged, or recently discharged, is the bastardized version of the Russian word *demobilizatsya*.

Under the rule of lawlessness in military units, senior enlisted personnel inevitably caused the large-scale hazing of junior enlisted men, which frequently resulted in injuries, murder and suicide. *Dedovshchina* was a small-scale replica of relations within the civilian Soviet society and had a devastating effect on the morale of conscripts in junior ranks.

Regardless of the horrific abuse and crimes perpetrated, or committed by *ded*-s against their younger comrades in arms, their *dembel* uniforms serve as a lasting memento of a past era.

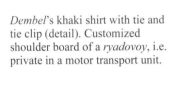

Dembel's khaki shirt with tie and tie clip (detail). Customized shoulder board of a *ryadovoy*, i.e. private in a motor transport unit.

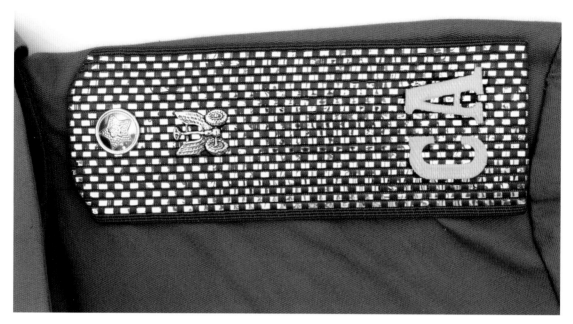

Dembel's khaki shirt (detail). Unique, silver thread woven shoulder board bearing the "vehicle wheels with steering gear and wings" badge of Motor Transport and Military Road units. It is an extraordinary *dembel* item, absolutely one of a kind.

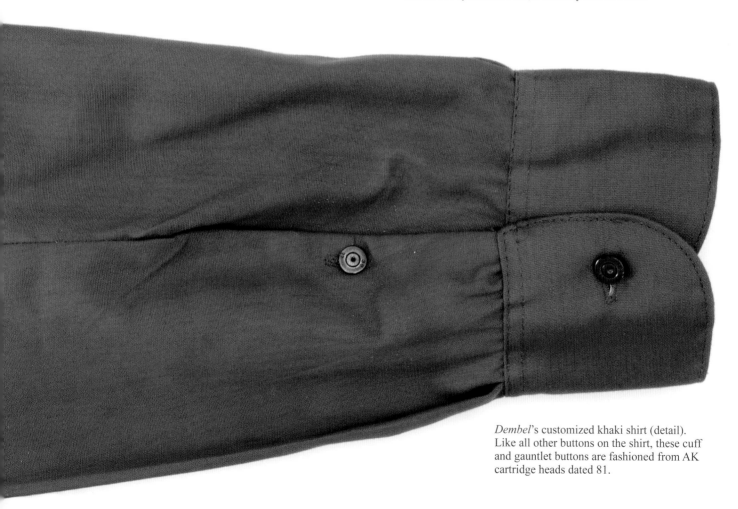

Dembel's customized khaki shirt (detail). Like all other buttons on the shirt, these cuff and gauntlet buttons are fashioned from AK cartridge heads dated 81.

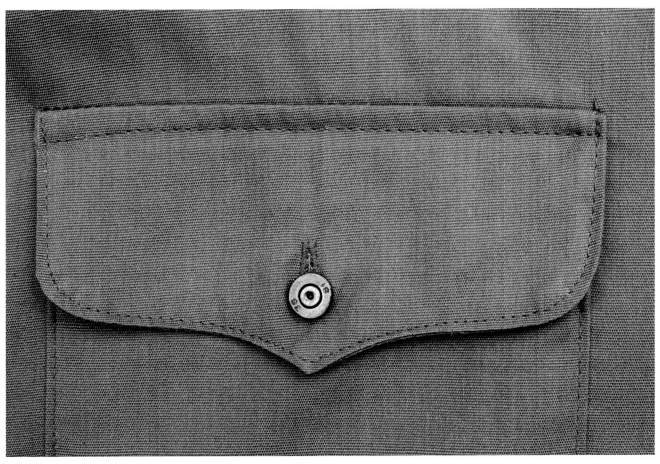

Dembel's customized khaki shirt (detail). The
breast pocket button is fashioned from an AK
cartridge head dated 81.

76. COMBAT ENGINEER/SAPPER SERGEANT *DEMBEL'S* CUSTOMIZED UNIFORM AT THE END OF HIS TOUR IN AFGHANISTAN

Ushankah fur hat with "Wreathed Red Star" EM's cap badge, M69 field uniform, customized sergeant's shoulder boards with lacquer coating on the three yellow ribbons, white parade belt with brass buckle. Also, EM grade khaki trousers without service-color stripes along the outer seams, tucked into high boots.

Combat engineer/sapper sergeant *dembel*'s customized M69 field uniform jacket with decorations and badges. There is no sewn-in collar liner.

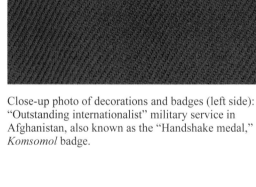

Close-up photo of decorations and badges, (right side):
Top row: Soldier-Sportsman badge, Grade I, Army
EM's Qualifications Badge, Grade 1, Outstanding
Soldier badge.
Middle row: "GTO"/Prepared for Labor and Defense/
badge, Grade II.
Bottom row: "For Mine Clearing" badge, which was
awarded to combat engineers/sappers for mine
clearing operations under combat conditions.

Close-up photo of decorations and badges (left side):
"Outstanding internationalist" military service in
Afghanistan, also known as the "Handshake medal,"
Komsomol badge.

Award document issued to an "Outstanding internationalist" who completed his military service in Afghanistan. The medal is also known as the "Handshake medal."

77. TWO-PIECE TTSKO THREE-COLOR CAMOUFLAGE PILOT UNIFORM, WITH ZSH-3 HELMET

Worn by a Vertolyotchick, Russian helicopter pilot, about to board a Mi-8 Helicopter, wearing a ZSh-3 hard shell helmet over his Shz-82 leather flying helmet, *Telnyashka* t-shirt, and a pair of *MOCKBA* brand sneakers

Helicopter pilot's ZSh-3 hard shell helmet worn over his ShZ-82 shearling-lined leather flying helmet with throat microphone attached. The two-piece head protection system of Soviet Air Force pilots and Army helicopter pilots comprised a padded aluminum shell with a tinted sun shield and a leather flying helmet with rubber-covered, internally wired earphones, a throat microphone, a sewn-on webbing chinstrap with a buckle to fasten the leather helmet and another chinstrap to attach the leather flight helmet to the outer hard shell.

The two-piece head protection system, (detail), the tinted sun shield is raised. A sewn-on webbing chinstrap with a buckle to fasten the ShZ-82 leather helmet and another chinstrap to attach the leather flight helmet to the ZSh-3 hard shell helmet are clearly visible.

The two-piece head protection system: padded aluminum shell with a tinted sun shield and a leather flying helmet. The leather-covered rib on top of the leather flight helmet fit into the notch inside the blue velvet-like liner of the outer hard shell and held the assembly in place.

ShL-82 summer leather flying helmet with rubber-covered, internally wired earphones, a throat microphone, and cables.

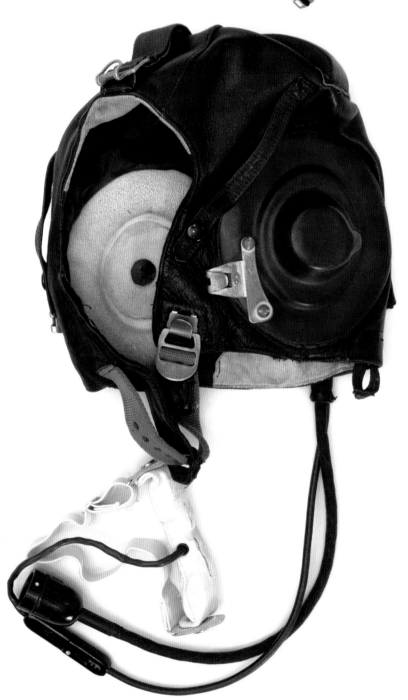

A pair of genuine Adidas "CAMPUS" shoes (left) and a pair of Soviet-made MOCKBA (Moscow in Russian) brand sneakers (right). The MOCKBA logo on the shoe tongues and the heels was a spitting image of the Trefoil "three-leaved plant" Adidas logo.

Similar to genuine and fake Adidas and Puma shoes, Soviet-made MOCKBA brand sneakers, actually locally manufactured ADIDAS clones, were extremely popular with the troops in Afghanistan and frequently replaced service-issue high boots and lace-up boots on field duty, (detail).

78. TWO-PIECE TTSKO THREE-COLOR CAMOUFLAGE PILOT UNIFORM, WITH ZSH-5 HELMET

In addition to the ZSh-3, the ZSh-5 helmet was the other service-issue helmet for Soviet helicopter crews and fighter pilots. The fiberglass helmet shell had permanent styrofoam and removable, Velcro-attached soft padding. The ZSh-5 was equipped with a pair of rather large, noise canceling earphones, which could be pulled aside with a string on either side when the pilot put the helmet on, or when he removed it. The ZSh-5 helmet had an air bladder in the nape area, which was inflated when the pilot was pulling high Gs and it also pressed the pilot's face against the oxygen mask.

The sun visor could be positioned manually, or it could be set to automatic. The visor went down with the touch of a button, or if the pilot activated the ejection seat. The integral earphones in the ZSh-5 and the microphone installed in the oxygen mask provided fighter pilots with a two-way communications capability. Helicopter crews had to use a throat mike.

Both the helmet and the mask had different versions, but in Afghanistan the most common fighter pilot configuration was the ZSh-5A helmet with the KM-34D oxygen mask.

Fighter pilot's ZSh-5A helmet with the KM-34D2 oxygen mask.

ZSh-5A helmet with the KM-34D2
oxygen mask (front view).

ZSh-5A helmet with the KM-34D2
oxygen mask (side view).

TTsKO three-color, camouflage pilot uniform jacket with zippered slash breast pockets and double D-ring fasteners on either side of the waistline.

TTsKO three-color camouflage pilot uniform jacket with concealed ventilation slits across the back, the integral Makarov pistol holster is clearly visible on the left-hand side (inside view detail). First pattern pilot camo jackets had a mesh insert under the arms, which were discontinued in early 1989. Such armpit vents allowed for maximum airflow and were supposed to keep pilots less sweaty. The manufacturer's date (89) and size stamp on the integral Makarov pistol holster is clearly visible.

TTsKO three-color, camouflage pilot uniform trousers with suspenders (side view). Knife pocket on the right hand side with *stroporez* parachute line cutter switchblade knife attached with an integral string.

TTsKO three-color, camouflage pilot uniform trousers with suspenders (front view). Slash hip pockets and zippered thigh pockets are clearly visible.

79. RED BANNER WITH THE HAMMER AND SICKLE INSIGNIA

Silk Soviet award flag to "Champions of Building Communism" are displayed in parades and are held by standard bearers. Heavy aluminum flag topper on the flag mast at left, and nickel-plated pressed steel topper at right.

The Moral Codex of Builders of Communism. A set of twelve codified moral rules are displayed on a red silk flag. Moral Code No.12. was, "Brotherly solidarity with the working people of all countries and with all peoples." The deployment of a "limited contingent" of Soviet troops to perform their internationalist mission in Afghanistan was the expression and practical implementation of such brotherly solidarity.

The image and the signature of Vladimir Ilyich Lenin, the father of communism, the leader of the 1917 Revolution in Russia, and the first premier of the USSR, adorn the silk Soviet award flag to champions of building Communism.

Red banner with the hammer and sickle insignia, manufacturer's date stamp (1986) is clearly visible, (detail). Close-up view of heavy aluminum flag topper and nickel plated pressed steel flagpole toppers.

80. M69 FIELD SERVICE UNIFORM IN FULL SUMMER MARCHING ORDER

Traffic controller on a desert road uses signal flags to indicate directions to armored convoys. He wears an *Afganka*, a.k.a. *Panamka* hat.

The *Veshmeshok* rucksack has its own canvas harness with a breast strap and is carried over the load bearing harness and equipment attached to the army belt. The *plash palatka* rain cape/ground sheet is rolled and is strapped onto the *veshmeshok.* The design of the *veshmeshok* rucksack remained unchanged for decades. On the newer version the canvas webbing straps, holding the *plash palatka* rain cape/ground sheet, were replaced with nylon webbing straps and a name tag holder with a small transparent window was added to the front. By the time of the Afghan war the *veshmeshok* was considered to be rather outdated and combat troops in Afghanistan preferred much larger and more comfortable private purchase rucksacks, or parachute bags to carry their heavy and bulky gear.

Close-up photo of an *Afganka*, a.k.a. *Panamka* hat. The manufacturer's date (83) and size stamp is clearly visible. Until 1989 the oiled canvas/simulated leather sweatband in service-issue Soviet headgear, including EM's grade and officers' grade peaked caps, field service hats and pilotka hats was almost always grey. The square-shaped piece of oiled canvas/simulated leather over the sweatband in the front of the hat was supposed to cover the pins of the cap badge and to protect the wearer's head from the sharp ends of the two pins that were folded in opposite directions.

Signal flags; battlefield relics.

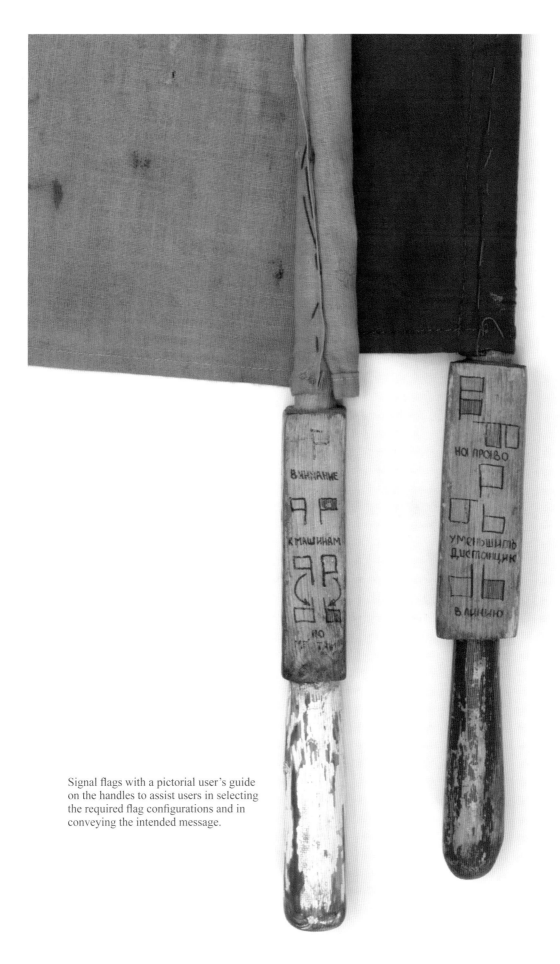

Signal flags with a pictorial user's guide on the handles to assist users in selecting the required flag configurations and in conveying the intended message.

81. *TELNYASHKA* SHIRT, LIGHT-WEIGHT INDIGO BLUE COTTON SHORTS AND VIETNAMESE-MADE RUBBER SANDALS

A horizontally striped light blue and white *telnyashka* shirt may have long sleeves, or may be a sleeveless vest. The *telnyashka* shirt became an iconic piece of Soviet military uniform design. While *telnyashka* shirts with stripes in different colors are part of the navy and the border guard uniforms, primarily it is the Airborne troops' light (VDV) blue and white striped *telnyashka* that is regarded as a mark of its wearer's elite status.

Since neither the M69, nor the M88 field service uniform configurations comprised any conventional shirts,

the light blue and white striped *telnyashka* shirt worn as a stand-alone item, or worn under the unbuttoned neck, or the open front of a field jacket, or worn along with a special uniform item, such as a *Mabuta*, or *Gorka* jacket, a *KLMK*, or a *KZS* cammo suit, a *TTsKO*, or a *Spetsodezhda* camouflage uniform, frequently showed up on Afghan war-period photos, except for winter scenes where heavy flannel undergarments and knitted sweaters were preferred to the *telnyashka*, which also had a good reputation as a "body warmer."

82. AIRCRAFT MECHANIC'S DESERT SAND COLOR TWO-PIECE WORK UNIFORM

With matching amber yellow felt beret, and Puma sneakers.

Air Force ground crew member's desert sand color two-piece work uniform jacket, ventilation holes under the sleeves, drawstring around the waistline. No cap badge is attached to the amber yellow felt beret, the manufacturer's date (88) and size stamp is clearly visible.

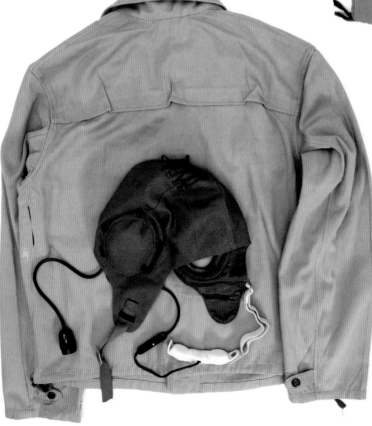

Air Force ground crew member's desert sand color, two-piece work uniform jacket, rear view. Concealed ventilation slits across the back are similar to those on the TTsKO camo pilot's jacket. There is an air force ground crew member's noise canceling canvas helmet with internally wired earphones and throat microphone on the jacket.

Puma "TOP WINNER" sneakers. Soviet soldiers loved genuine and fake Adidas and Puma sports shoes and frequently substituted bulky and uncomfortable service-issue footwear with private-purchase sneakers.

Air Force ground crew member's desert sand color, two-piece work uniform trousers. Thigh pockets with concealed button closure, integral cloth straps and pressed steel buckles to adjust the waist, and adjusting tabs with snap fasteners on the trouser cuffs are clearly visible.

Chaderi, a.k.a. *burqa*, made of rayon fabric, (detail). Machine-embroidered head and upper torso portions of a Pakistani-made blue *chaderi* with integral concealing net, or grille in front of the eyes of its wearer, genuine Afghani tribal jewelry.

Inside view of a *chaderi* (detail),
close-up photo of the concealing net, or
grille in front of the wearer's eyes.

"Inside looking out" view of the world (actually
an Afghani postcard showing a market scene)
through the concealing net, or grille in front of
the wearer's eyes.

Close-up photo of an anklet, or ankle ring with black velvet
lining. Sadly enough, such pieces of Afghani tribal jewelry are
more frequently seen these days on *bacha baazi* dancing boys
entertaining all-male audiences.

84. *CHADERI*-CLAD AFGHANI MOTHERS

With their young daughters in locally-made traditional tribal clothes.

Outfit for a little girl. This richly ornamented silk *shalwar kameez* would fit a two- or three-year-old little girl. It was a generous gift from a friendly carpet merchant in Mazar-e Sharif, Balkh Province in 2011.

Another richly ornamented silk dress, which would fit a five, or six-year-old little girl.

Locally made leather shoes for a lady.

Two traditional Afghani dresses for little girls.

85. AFGHANI FAMILY

Man in a *wahskat*, a.k.a. "photographer's vest," over a *shalwar kameez*, *shemagh* around his neck, *sindhi* cap, locally made leather sandals. He is accompanied by two *chaderi*-clad ladies and children.

Sindhi cap and *shemagh*.

An assortment of *shemagh* shawls.

Sindhi cap, front view.

Shalwar kameez with a few Afghani banknotes in the side pocket of the loose fitting *kameez* shirt.

86. INSURGENT IN TRADITIONAL LOCAL CLOTHES

Chinese-made chest rig worn over a *kameez* and under the "fishing vest,"
a.k.a. "photographer's vest."

Such vests with a host of pockets of different shapes and sizes, some with zippered, some with buttoned, some with Velcro closure, are extremely popular with men wearing traditional clothes and are quite common in Afghanistan.

This photo demonstrates that in Afghanistan there is only a thin line of distinction between a peaceful civilian, like the father in the previous photograph, and an armed combatant, like this man.

Two different qualities and types of *patoo*, which is a heavy woolen blanket, or shawl. The bottom one is made of much finer wool and is ornamented with sophisticated embroidery, the one on top is a common type made of a cheaper material, but it is more suitable for everyday wear.

Sindhi cap, overhead view. The cap is studded with small glass beads and is embroidered.

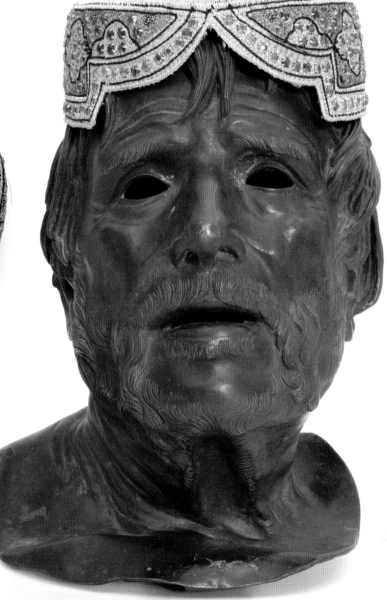

Sindhi cap, front view.

Chinese-made chest rig (detail), Soviet-made F-1 hand grenade in one grenade pocket and a spare UZRGM-1 fuse in small inside pocket.

Differences in the floor plates of AK-47 magazines in a three-cell Chinese-made chest rig. Soviet-made 'bakelite' AKM 7.62 x 39 mm thirty-round magazine (left), Chinese-made pressed steel plate AK (Type-56 Assault Rifle) magazine with circular "Made in China" stamp, which suggests that this magazine must have been intended for the commercial market (center), and standard Soviet-made steel magazine (right). The "Made in China" stamp suggests that the Chinese magazine was originally intended for export and not for service in the PLA.

Chinese-made chest rig, loaded with grenades and magazines, with an Afghan insurgent's "safari vest" under it.

Close-up photograph of loaded AK magazines placed on a three-cell Chinese-made chest rig. Soviet-made bakelite AKM 7.62 x 39 mm thirty-round magazine (left), Chinese-made pressed steel plate AK (Type-56 Assault Rifle) magazine (center), and standard Soviet-made steel magazine (right).

87. MERCHANT IN AN AFGHANI MARKET

With a tin can of Soviet caviar in his hand, which was still available at affordable prices even in the last few days before the total withdrawal of Soviet troops on February 15, 1989.

The merchant is wearing white *lungee* and a tailor-made black *wahskat*, or waistcoat, over his *shalwar kameez*, which has the traditional mandarin collar. Only a few rounds of ammunition in a fabric cartridge loop strip sewn on the front strap of his shoulder holster are visible. Although he is packing a brand new, 1989-dated Soviet Makarov pistol, only the spare ammo in neat elastic loops is sticking out from under the waistcoat.

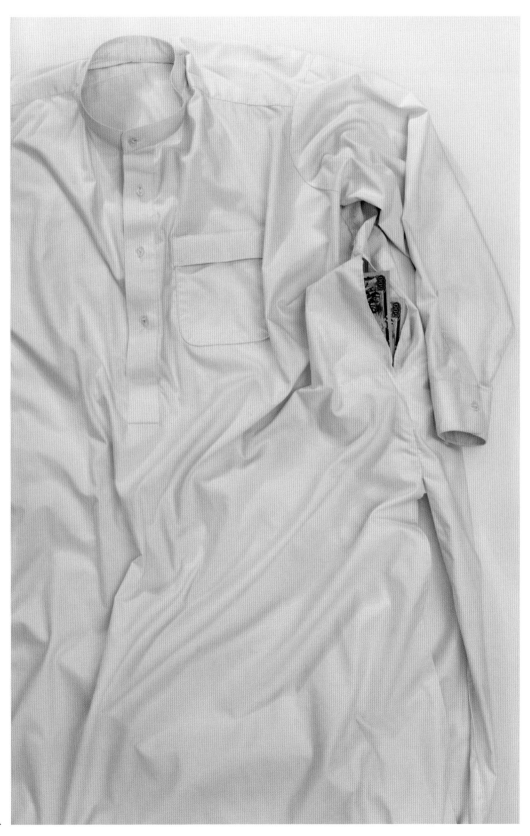

Kameez (detail), with the traditional mandarin collar and a few Afghani banknotes in the side pocket.

Shalwar.

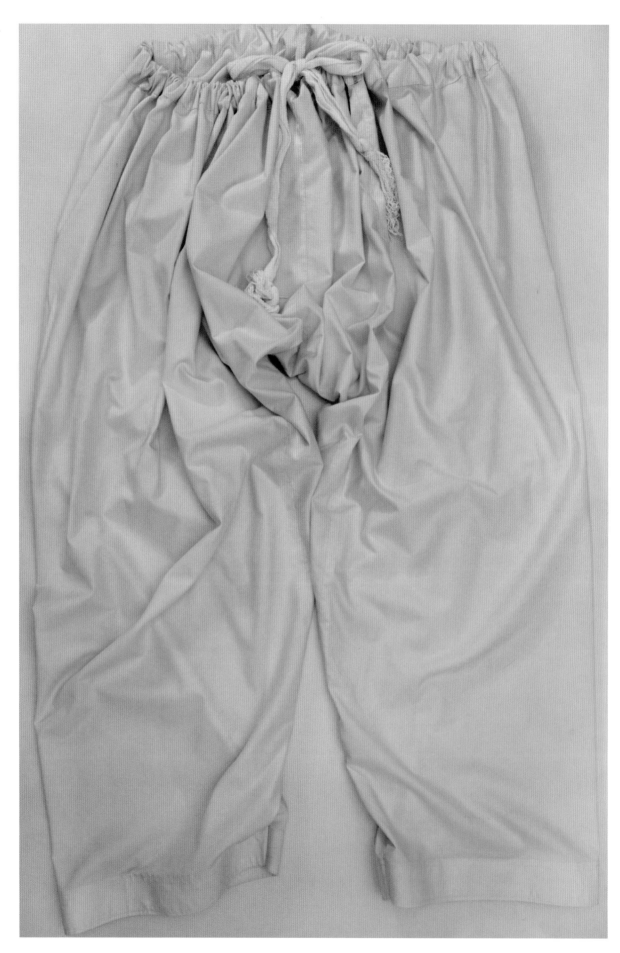

Shalwar (detail), the loose fitting trousers were tied around the waist with a length of loosely woven gauze strip.

Soviet soldiers who performed their internationalist duty in Afghanistan gained quite a bit of notoriety for selling Afghans, including individuals, village elders, market traders, Mujahid warriors, and warlords, virtually everything that was not bolted to the concrete floor in their barracks, from Soviet confectionery and vodka to their uniforms and ammunition to weapons and vehicles either in spare parts, or as a whole.

Their presence gave a real boost to the economy of the whole region and offered hefty benefits to traders and dealers not only in the "*Brezhnev Bazaar*" and in the Chicken Street flea market in downtown Kabul, but in small rural communities in Afghanistan as well as in faraway places, like Peshawar on the Pakistani side of the border, where the same Soviet specialty products, including vodka and caviar, were readily available for roughly the same price as in the Afghan capital city.

White *lungee*, twenty-four inches long, in lighter, but somewhat thicker turban cloth.

Tin box of Soviet caviar.

Tailor-made *wahskat*, or waistcoat made by a tailor in Pul-e Khumri, Baghlan Province in late 2008. While there are buttons on the right-hand side, no buttonholes were placed on the left side, since a waistcoat is supposed to be worn open over the loose-fitting *kameez* shirt. The big advantage of a waistcoat made to measure, like this is that the zippered left inside pocket doubles up as an integral pistol holster.

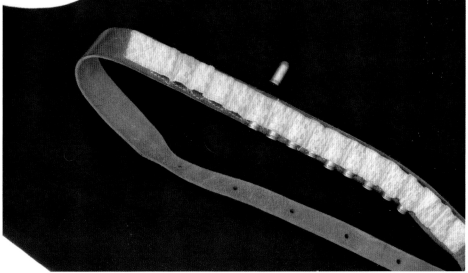

9x18 mm Makarov ammunition in an elastic fabric cartridge loop strip sewn on the front strap of a locally made shoulder holster.

88. SOVIET CHEST RIG

Worn over *Gorka* suit.

In the initial years of the war only standard, service-issue belt-mounted three-pocket and four-pocket ammunition pouches, or captured Chinese-made chest rigs were available to Soviet soldiers, who acquired a taste for the Chinese chest rigs of Mujahideen warriors before long. Additionally, a vast variety of "rigger-made" *lifchiks* (lit.: bra in Russian) were used by extremely inventive combat troops in Afghanistan. *Lifchik* was army slang, more formally they used '*nagrudnik*', or simply '*razgruzka*' for chest-mounted ammunition pouches. The first Soviet Army-issue chest rigs entered active duty with the troops towards the middle of the war and these were copies of the Chinese chest rigs. However, the wooden peg and matching canvas loop closure on the pockets and flaps of these very early Soviet models were abandoned on the first service-issue Soviet chest rigs, which used both Velcro hook and loop fasteners and snap fasteners on the magazine and grenade pockets. Chinese-made

chest rigs were designed to hold one magazine in each of the three, or four mag pockets and Soviet soldiers had to soak these chest rigs in water and use brute force to insert two magazines in each cell to make the pockets a bit wider to accommodate two AK magazines each. Nevertheless, they still remained very tight for two mags. The Soviet-made chest rig had wider pockets to hold two AK magazines in each cell.

There is no way of telling whether this is a Soviet service-issue chest rig, or it was made, maybe repaired locally. The rare horizontal arrangement of the grenade pockets appears on an original snapshot of a Soviet soldier in Afghanistan. All I know about this chest rig is that it must have been kept in storage for over twenty years, since it was issued to an Afghani Local Police officer in Baghlan Province as part of his kit. I bought it from him in 2010.

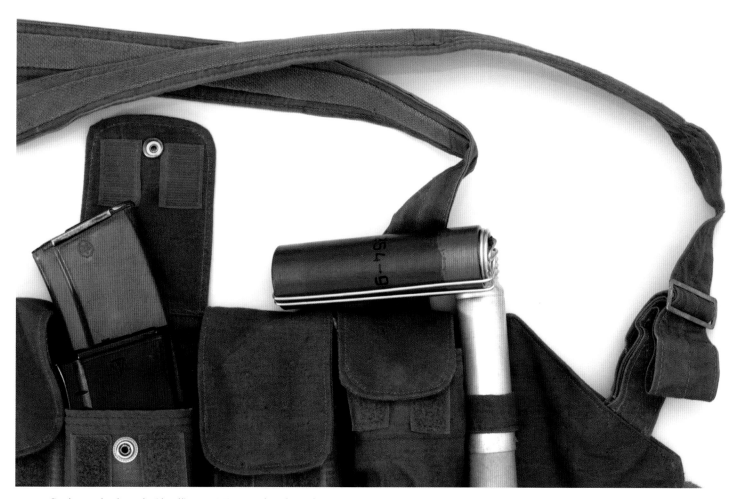

Soviet-made chest rig (detail), two AK magazines in each pocket, matching Velcro hook and loop fasteners plus snap fasteners on magazine pocket and flap. NSP smoke grenade attached to shoulder strap.

NSP smoke grenade/ground signal patron.

Soviet-made chest rig (detail), webbing
strap reinforced shoulder strap.

Soviet-made chest rig (detail), D-ring to receive the snap hook at the end of the adjustable webbing waist strap, 30 mm signal flare held tight by a cloth loop and an open pocket at the bottom, matching Velcro hook and loop fasteners plus snap fasteners on grenade pocket and flap.

89. TRADITIONAL, DECORATIVE WOVEN CAMEL BAGS

Hold crated ammunition for Mujahid warriors.

Weapons, ammunition, and supplies for Mujahid warriors had to be carried on camels, donkeys, and mules and even horses over treacherous mountain passes and dangerous open terrain all the way from Pakistan to different provinces of Afghanistan. Hosts of pack animals were employed to transport large amounts of supplies across the country and caravans were always exposed to the watchful eyes of Soviet aircrews and ground observers.

Cargo bags for a camel, front panel with large metal rings to attach the bag to the saddle (detail).

Cargo bags for a camel, side panel with large metal
rings to attach the bag to the saddle (detail).

The *shotur khoorgeen*, i.e. a pair of cargo bags for a camel. They were acquired near Bay Saqal, Baghlan Province in 2007.

"In the dim light at dawn the fourth man, who had been left behind by mistake, regained consciousness. He did not know where he was, where the smoke and the stench of burning flesh were coming from, nor did he recall what actually had happened to him.

"He tried several times, but his feet got entangled in the old *shotur khoorgeen* on which he had been lying like a log. Luckily, he could not see his own face, which was quite disfigured by the impression of a rusty iron ring on the *khoorgeen*. He tripped and stumbled, but he managed to stand up at last …"
—Excerpt from *Zarbalistan* by Zammis Schein

The pair of saddlebags for a donkey holds fully loaded
AK magazines for the Mujahideen.

Another *khoorgeen*, namely cargo bag is decorated with
helicopters, a quadruple-barreled—assumedly—ZPU-4
anti-aircraft machine gun, soldiers on foot as well as on
top of tracked armored personnel carriers.

A pair of traditional tribal design saddle bags with military motifs.

INDEX

Also by Zammis Schein

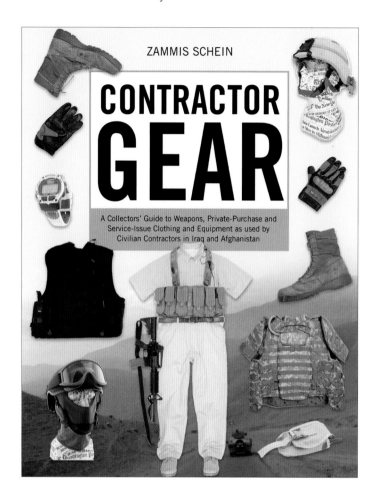

CONTRACTOR GEAR

A Collectors' Guide to Weapons, Private-Purchase

and Service-Issue Clothing and Equipment

as Used by Civilian Contractors in Iraq and Afghanistan

Zammis Schein

This book is a comprehensive collectors' guide to Operation Enduring Freedom (OEF), and Operation Iraqi Freedom (OIF) civilian contractors private-purchase and service-issue clothing, equipment, and weapons as they were worn and used in the field between 2002 and 2014.
Size: 8½"x11" • 550 color photos • 256 pp
ISBN: 978-0-7643-5258-4 • hard cover • $59.99